PSYCHIC AWAKENING

A BEGINNER'S GUIDE TO DEVELOPING YOUR
INTUITIVE PSYCHIC ABILITIES, INCLUDING
CLAIRVOYANCE, MIND READING, MANIFESTATION,
ASTRAL PROJECTION, MEDIUMSHIP, AND SPIRIT
GUIDES

HARLOW WOLFE

HENTOPAN
PUBLISHING

CONTENTS

Special Offer From Hentopan Publishing

Get this additional book free just for joining the Hentopan Launch Squad.

Hundreds of others are already enjoying early access to all of our current and future books, 100% free.

If you want insider access, plus this free book, all you have to do is scan the code below with your phone!

INTRODUCTION

What do you believe? Do you believe there is a deep state? Do you believe there are UFOs? Do you believe there was a moon landing, or do you believe it was staged? There are certain things in life that we are unable to reach a consensus on. We either believe it, or we don't. Psychic powers fall into this category. There are those whose psychic powers are real, but some believe that being psychic is a bunch of nonsense. I can appreciate both sides of the argument, for that is the story of my life. My name is Harlow Wolfe and the topic of psychic powers has shaped my life for as long as I can remember.

Many years ago, I was a small child living in the St. Bernard Parish of New Orleans. My mother was a single parent and worked long hours to keep us fed. Fortunately, my grandparents lived just a block away, and I would spend my days with them while my mother was at work.

Though the neighborhood is largely Roman Catholic, there has always been a sizable part of the population that believes in voodoo and witchcraft. I was never exposed to these belief systems; however, I was exposed to psychic beliefs. My grandmother, Marie, did not hesitate to tell others that she had psychic powers.

There were numerous times during my childhood when I would hear Marie talking to someone in another room. The first time this happened, I went to investigate and found her alone in the room. I asked her who she had been talking to, and she smiled.

My grandmother told me that she was able to talk to people who were no longer on this Earth. She also told me that she knew things about other people that only they would know. She said she was able to do these things because she was psychic. At the time, I thought this was the coolest thing; my grandmother was psychic!

I remember asking Marie if I was a psychic too. She told me that I was and that there would come a time when I would know it. At the time, I did not believe her because I had never experienced any of the things that she had experienced.

When I turned 13 years old, my attitude to my grandmother changed. I stopped attributing her eccentric behavior to her being psychic. Instead, I began to believe that my grandmother had a psychological issue. It was a source of embarrassment for me, and I stopped bringing friends over to her home. I was positive that psychic powers did not exist. I believed that anyone claiming to having psychic powers simply had either an unsophisticated mind or psychological issues.

By the time I was 16, I was busy with school, playing sports, and dating girls. Because of this, I spent less time with my grandparents than when I was younger. Life was going great for me until the morning of July 10th, 1977. That was when my mother received a phone call from my grandmother. My grandfather George had passed away.

The news of his death hit me hard. While I loved both my grandparents, I was particularly close to George. From the time I was small, I can remember how being around him made me feel safe. I always felt like whatever was going on in my world, things would be alright.

The funeral was attended only by my grandmother, my mom, me, and a few of George's close friends. After the ceremony, we all went to my grandparents' home to console each other.

A few years passed, and I found myself very busy keeping up my grades in college and working. I had not seen my grandmother in a while, so one day I dropped by to see how she was doing. She welcomed me in, and made lunch for me. I sat in the kitchen and ate the sandwich she had made while she excused herself and went into another room.

About 15 minutes later, I heard her talking to someone. At first, I just ignored it, as she had been doing this since I was small. But then it occurred to me that maybe this time was different and that maybe she was having trouble coping with the death of her husband and had reached a breaking point. I was concerned and went to her.

When I reached the room, something told me that I should stop and listen to what she was saying instead of walking in right away. It did not take long before I felt the sadness well up within me. I realized that she was talking to my grandfather, George. I walked in to comfort her but was stopped in my tracks by what I saw. She was smiling at me! I was confused by the peaceful look on her face.

Sensing my confusion, Marie told me that everything was OK. She shared with me that she had talked to George and had been doing so since his passing. She hugged and as she held me, she told me that I should develop my psychic powers. At that moment, I knew that my grandmother could sense my sadness. Though I was doing well at school and work, something was missing in my life. I was not happy, and she knew it.

I told her that I did not believe in psychic powers.

"Just try it, Harlow; what do you have to lose? Surely, you want more for your life," she said with an all-knowing look in her eyes.

At that moment, I began to wonder if my grandmother knew something about me that I did not. *Is it possible that I do have psychic powers?* I wondered. She said it would take time to develop my abilities and that I needed to trust in them. She compared developing psychic power to learning how to ride a bike. She told me there would be times I would fall until I learned to keep my balance.

That evening, I looked into my bathroom mirror as I brushed my teeth. Looking at my reflection, I came to realize that I was experiencing grief. I had never gotten over the grief of losing my grandfather. Our connection had been so strong. He had always been my rock. Because of his advanced age, his death should not have been unexpected. Yet, I was having trouble dealing with his loss. My grandmother, on the other hand, whom I had thought was crazy for her beliefs in psychic powers, seemed sincerely happy. It was then that I decided to take her advice more seriously.

I used every chance I had to learn more about psychic powers. I read about them extensively, and I applied to my life what I learned. I was surprised by how quickly I started to get results. Long story short, I have been actively learning about psychic powers for more than thirty years.

At some point I began using my psychic abilities to help others, just as my grandmother had helped me. At first, I only helped a few people, but the number of people seeking my help continued to grow. I eventually became an energy healer. I also taught others to develop their own innate psychic powers.

This book was written in the spirit of my need to help others. I have included the information and techniques that allowed me to cultivate my psychic abilities. It's written for anyone who is like I was in my younger years who is curious about their psychic powers and would like to develop them.

1

THE PSYCHIC WORLD

If you are reading this book, you probably are curious about psychic powers. You may be wondering if you possess them or believe that you have them and want to develop them. If any of these statements are true, this book is for you. Before we go any further with this chapter, I invite you to answer the following questions:

- Have you ever thought of someone, only to have them call you shortly afterward?
- Have you ever heard your telephone ring, and had a feeling that you knew who was calling?
- Have you ever thought of someone you have not heard from for some time, only to have them contact you out of the blue?
- Have you ever come up with a creative idea or the

solution to a problem that has been eluding seemingly out of the blue?

- Have you ever been going about your day when out of the blue you receive a message from within, telling you that you need to follow up on something you have not previously given your attention to?
- Have you ever encountered someone for the first time and had an instant liking for them?
- Have you ever encountered someone for the first time and instantly felt connected to them?
- Have you ever encountered someone for the first time, and instantly had a bad feeling about them?
- Have you ever experienced an inner voice telling you what you should do, though there was nothing in your reality to support that thought?
- Have you ever entered a room and instantly had a good or bad feeling about it?

These questions illustrate common situations that we all experience in our lives that indicate psychic powers. And this is merely a short list of examples of psychic powers. The challenge for many of us is that when we experience these things, we often attribute it to coincidence. Or because they seem insignificant, we do not find them worthy of our attention.

Yes, when you have a "gut feeling," or you say, "Something is telling me to...," you are experiencing psychic powers. When you say, "I had a feeling that would happen," you are experiencing a form of psychic powers!

OK, here is the big reveal: Everyone has psychic powers! Being psychic is a natural part of who we are. We were born with it. Unfortunately, most of us are unaware of our psychic abilities, so we never develop them. As my grandmother told me, learning to use your psychic abilities is like learning how to ride a bicycle. Most of us are unaware of our psychic abilities for several reasons.

First, we have created stereotypes of those who have psychic abilities. They are people who look into crystal balls or read tarot cards and tell us our future. We also may think that psychic powers are not real, just a form of quackery. This is understandable because there are some who victimize others by claiming to be fortunetellers and charging them for a reading.

A second reason we are unaware of our psychic abilities is because of our societal indoctrination. We live in a culture that prioritizes the physical realm over the spiritual realm. This is understandable, given the way we view ourselves and our world. From the time we are children, the overriding message we receive is that we need to get an education and graduate, then go to work.

At work, we learn that we must produce in order to remain employed. As consumers, we often fall victim to comparing ourselves with others. We are also flooded with advertisers' messages about what car we should be driving, what clothes we should wear, what beverages we should drink, or what credit card we should have.

Even the way that we perceive ourselves is heavily influenced by the traditional perspective of science. We have learned to understand ourselves as a physical body with a mind. Though we have learned a great deal about the human body and psychology, there remains the difficult question of consciousness. What is consciousness? Where is it found? How does it work? So far, Western science has offered no answers.

I am reminded of a story about a man who drives into a parking lot at night. The parking lot is only half-lit because the lighting on one side is not working. The man parks on the dark side. He gets out of his car and walks toward his destination. While on the dark side of the parking lot, he drops his keys.

Meanwhile, another man sees the first man searching the illuminated side of the parking lot. Figuring that the man has lost something, the second man goes to offer his help. Time passes while both men search, but no keys are recovered.

The second man asks the first man, "Where did you last see your keys?" The first man points to the dark half of the parking lot. "If you lost your keys on that side of the parking lot, why are you looking for them on this side?" asks the second man. The first man replies, "Because it is easier to look for them on the side that is lit.

Just like the first man, we as a society have chosen to focus on the physical realm. The nature of consciousness is like those lost keys. Since it exists beyond the light of our understanding, we have chosen to focus on the world of physicality. We have avoided exploring the dark side of the parking lot.

More profoundly, our focus on the physical realm has also shaped our perception of how we see ourselves. Our sense of self has been associated with our mind and body. Most of us believe that what defines us is what we think, what we feel, and our physical body. Further, we believe consciousness is something that exists within our brains. Because we experience ourselves as a physical self, we perceive everything outside of us as separate. It is this sense of separateness that creates the ego.

The Illusions of Our Minds

What is the universe? However we define it, we believe that we are located in it, as is everything else we experience. Whether it is galaxies, oceans, or a blade of grass, all of these things appear to be separate from ourselves. However, our sense of separateness and physicality are illusionary. To begin with, no universe exists outside of us. As quantum physics has demonstrated, everything that exists is, at the most fundamental level, energy.

We perceive that the universe is an extension of the same energy field of which we are comprised. If the universe was a pool of water, each of us would be a drop merging with that water. The illusions that we experience, such as a universe outside ourselves, are created by the mind.

Since the advent of Newtonian physics, scientists have considered matter to be the building block of the physical world. With all their references to matter, scientists have yet to prove its existence beyond their mental concept. In the same way, no one has ever proven the existence of a thought other than our concept of it.

All of us have experienced thoughts, but has anyone ever found a thought? Has anyone located where thoughts arise from or discovered what they are made of? Most of humanity has fallen for the superstition of materialism. Just as there is no supporting evidence that black cats are bad luck, so it is true that no one has offered any evidence for the existence of matter or thoughts. All that can be said is that we have mental concepts of these things.

The only thing that we can be sure of is that we have an awareness of physical objects and thoughts; however, we lack knowledge of these things. In fact, we lack any knowledge of anything that we experience. After all, knowledge is experienced as a thought, but what is a thought?

Any attributions to the nature of the universe, including ourselves, are all conceptual. Meaning anything that we experience is a construct of our mind. Unknowingly, we project our concepts onto that which we are experiencing. This process of projecting concepts onto our experience is exactly what happens when we dream at night.

When dreaming, your dream self inhabits a dream world. The dream self, which is your sense of self, actively engages with this dream world, fully accepting its world as reality. Unless you are lucid dreaming, your dream self cannot perceive that it, and its dream world, are merely projections of the one having the dream.

Dreams are mental concepts that are projected by the mind. What substance are dreams made of? Has anyone collected this substance for analysis? Of course not! Our dreams are a perfect metaphor for an alternative explanation to what we experience in our physical existence. Could not our daily experience of reality be the projection of the mind as well? Could not the same be true of us?

Whether it is a dream that we are experiencing while sleeping or the "reality" that we experience in the waking state, there is one thing that we can be certain of. We are aware of both the dream and the waking state. Awareness is the force that brings to life all that we experience. Without awareness, there can be no experience.

This is why you and the universe are not separate entities. Both you and the universe are brought into existence by awareness. But whose awareness makes this possible? This awareness that I am pointing to does not belong to anyone or anything. Rather, awareness is an entity unto itself. We and all that we experience are its manifestations, and all of existence is found within it.

The Oneness of Existence

It was once believed that the atom was a solid structure that contained subatomic particles. It is now known that neither the atom nor its subatomic particles are solid; instead, they are made of energy. Everything that we experience, at the most fundamental level, is made of energy.

You are not only a manifestation of this energy; you are inseparable from it. Like a drop that is removed from the ocean, the drop shows no resemblance to the mighty ocean, but the drop and the ocean are identical in their chemical composition. It is only our minds that make distinctions between these two. In the same way, you are inseparable from the universe.

Instead of focusing on the physicality of life and your sense of separateness, I encourage you to challenge your preconceived notions of reality. Consider the possibility that you are part of an energetic system from which you create your experiences, which is the subject of the next section.

The Greater Consciousness System

Your life and all that you experience are part of a conscious energy system. This system encompasses all that is. There is a continuous flow of energy in this system, which creates the manifestations of existence. It is the manifestation process that leads to the expansion of consciousness.

In this system, there is the unmanifested and the manifested. The unmanifested is the realm of pure consciousness. Pure consciousness is the most fundamental aspect of the manifested realm; its qualities include wholeness, oneness, timelessness, unboundedness, and infinite potentiality for expression.

By manifesting into form, consciousness learns about itself, resulting in the creation of new expressions of itself. Our connection with pure consciousness is restricted in our manifested form because the world of form monopolizes our attention. This obsession with the world of form is not a mistake; rather, it allows us to have experiences.

We can think of the conscious energy system like a video game. When you play a video game, you, the gamer, are represented by an avatar interacting with its virtual environment. By interacting with its environment, the avatar can accumulate points and move to the next level, or it can be killed off and start over.

Your avatar is restricted in what it can do by a rule set programmed into the game. If not for this rule set, playing the game would be impossible because there would be too much information to consider. How would you navigate your avatar if there were no guidelines or limits?

To illustrate this, here is another computer analogy. You can chat online and converse with another user with relative ease.

You type your message, and it is formatted on the screen so that the other user can read it. In turn, the other user responds to you by following the same procedure.

While you are chatting with the other user, hundreds of conversations are simultaneously being carried out by other users. What if the rule set that isolates your conversation from all the other users did not exist? It would be impossible to make sense of your conversation with all the other conversations flooding your screen.

Your essential self, pure consciousness, is like the gamer, while your manifested self is like the avatar. Your experience of this physical realm is like the avatar's experience of its cyber world. And just as the avatar cannot know the gamer, you cannot know your essential self experientially. However, you can know it intuitively.

Just as the avatar and the gamer are intimately connected, so are you and your essential self. Further, any limitations you may perceive are rule sets that allow you to make sense of your experience. You are here to have a human experience to score points and move to the next level. How do you score points? You raise the vibrational frequency of your life's energy. What happens when you move to the next level? You raise your level of consciousness.

Raising the level of consciousness is the purpose of our existence. However, the purpose of raising your level of consciousness is not for your benefit alone. It is for the benefit of all living things. By raising your vibrational level, you affect the vibration of all other beings. You ultimately win the game by contributing to the rise of the collective consciousness. Before you can raise your vibrational level, you first need to understand this energy field. Learning to develop your psychic powers first requires preparing yourself, which is the topic of the next chapter.

2

LAYING THE GROUNDWORK

I stated earlier that most of us are unaware of our psychic abilities because we do not consider them. Normally, when we experience our psychic abilities, we attribute them to coincidence or an overactive imagination.

Maybe I am thinking of a friend I have not seen in a while, and minutes later, he calls me. I tell myself it's a coincidence. I may suddenly feel that something will go wrong with the project I am working on. Sure enough, something goes wrong. In both situations, I have not connected to my psychic powers because I either forget about my premonitions or consider them coincidental.

This is why one of the most important things you can do to prepare yourself for developing your psychic abilities is to track your experiences and see if you can discern a pattern. The best way of doing this is through journaling.

By keeping a daily journal, you can look back and identify those situations where the message you received accurately foretold subsequent events. One of the best ways to start off journaling is to write about your dreams.

Dream Journal

Your dreams are representations of your subconscious thoughts. In turn, your thoughts, both conscious and subconscious, are bits of information from the data streams found within consciousness. When you have a dream, you experience this data as symbols that are meaningful to you. That is what psychic powers are; information received by us that is not detectable by our five senses.

We live in an information-rich universe. Most of us are only aware of the information that we receive through our five senses. We take in information from seeing it, hearing it, smelling it, touching it, and tasting it. However, a lot of information eludes us because it can only be detected mentally. We are all able to detect information mentally, meaning that we all have psychic abilities, but to be psychic is to become aware of this ability. Our dreams are the psychic information that we are most familiar with.

Following are some tips for journaling your dreams:

1. Keep a journal and pen by your bedside. Every
   morning when you wake up, record the dreams you
   had the night before. If you did not have a dream or
   forgot it, notate that in your journal.
2. Before falling asleep each night, have the intention that
   you will remember your dreams when you wake up the
   following morning. One way of doing this is repeating
   to yourself, "I will remember my dreams" until you fall
   asleep. You will more likely remember your dreams if
   you declare this intention.
3. When learning to record your dreams, be patient with
   yourself. It takes time to get into the habit of
   consistently recording dreams. It also takes time to
   improve your ability to recall your dreams. It is
   common to remember only parts of your dream. As
   recording your dreams becomes a habit, you will
   gradually increase your ability to remember them.

As your dream journaling becomes a part of your morning
routine, you will discover that your dreams will become more
detailed, and you will have an easier time remembering them.
Combined with the other psychic development work you will
be learning, your dream journaling will lead you to develop
greater awareness of your precognitive dreams; those that foretell the future.

You will be able to identify your precognitive dreams after journaling for a month or so. Review your dream journal and see if you can find any dreams you had that came true. When you have identified these precognitive dreams, look for patterns among those dreams. Are there certain dream characters that repeatedly appear? Is there a common tone or feeling that you get from these dreams, or is there a common theme?

When you can identify the patterns, you will be able to experiment with future dreams. If the dream fits the pattern, does it accurately foretell the future? The main thing is to have fun with dream journaling and the other psychic development work you will learn about in this book. Be dedicated to your psychic development work but do not take it too seriously if things do not go as you hoped.

The purpose of dream journaling and other development work is to help you gain control of your natural ability. Like anything else in life, developing one's ability takes continued practice and refinement. It should be noted that dream journaling will open the flood gates of your psychic powers, so do not be surprised if you experience more than just dreams. You may experience visits from the spirit world or a deceased loved one.

Psychic Journal

As with dream journals, psychic journals are used to record your experiences so that you can learn to identify patterns that point to your psychic skills. Each day, record in your journal any unusual experiences that you have. Examples of unusual experiences include things like gut feelings, apparent coincidences, inner voices, or hearing voices from beyond. Review your journal after writing for a month or so to see if your experiences foretold future events.

Throughout this book you will find exercises for you to do to strengthen your psychic abilities. I highly recommended that you document your experiences of these exercises in your psychic journal. Your journal will play a vital role in your psychic development.

Daily Meditation

The purpose of meditation is to redirect your attention from the outer world toward your inner world. Your outer world is a reflection or projection of your inner world; only when you understand your inner world can you move beyond the illusions of your mind. When you can get clarity about your inner world, you will be better prepared to use your psychic powers efficiently. There are some key points to keep in mind when learning how to meditate:

1. Maintain an attitude of total acceptance and non-judgment for everything you experience.
2. Do not try to control, change, or resist anything that you experience.
3. Allow all that you experience complete freedom to express itself.

4. When meditating, you may experience thoughts such as:

- My thoughts keep coming; they are not slowing down.
- This is too difficult.
- This is boring.
- I have more important things to do.
- This is not working.
- Am I doing this right?

Ignore these thoughts and continue to focus on the meditation.

Finally, there is no correct or incorrect way to meditate, as long as you allow yourself to witness all of your experiences. No thought or experience can affect you as long as you do not provide it with your attention. It is your attention to the phenomena within your mind that gives them their power. No thought or sensation inherently possesses its own power; its power is derived from your attention. Make a shift from giving thoughts your attention to simply being a silent witness to them.

The most basic meditation is breath meditation. Though simple, it is very effective in calming the mind.

Basic Meditation

1. Find a quiet location where you will not be disturbed.

Sit down, make yourself comfortable and allow
yourself to relax.

2. Close your eyes and just focus on your breath. Place
your awareness on your breath as you inhale, feel the
sensations of your breath as it enters your body, and as
it flows downward toward your lungs. When you
exhale, experience the sensations as your breath flows
upward toward your mouth and out of your body.

3. Continue to focus on the movement of your breath
with each inhalation and each exhalation.

4. When you experience yourself getting distracted by
thoughts, simply return your attention back to your
breathing. Regardless of how many times you lose your
concentration, just return your attention back to your
breath.

5. Do not, at any time, judge or criticize yourself or
anything that you experience. Being distracted by
thoughts is normal, and you have allowed yourself to
be distracted by your thoughts all your life. It takes
practice to discipline your mind.

By practicing meditation regularly, you will develop greater
awareness of when your mind becomes distracted. You will
realize it sooner each time you catch yourself and you will learn
to quiet your mind.

Mindfulness is related to meditation. While meditation usually
involves looking inward, mindfulness is about expanding your

awareness of what is occurring in your environment. Most of us go through our days trapped in our heads. The goal of mindfulness is to experience the world free of the filters created by thought.

Mindfulness

A man was walking along the side of a road when he saw a rider on a horse approaching him from a distance. As the rider got closer, the man could see that the rider was not controlling his horse. The rider tried to hold on as his horse galloped at full speed. When the rider was close enough, the man shouted out to him: "Where are you going?" The rider replied back: "I do not know. Ask the horse."

This story is a metaphor for the lives we lead. The rider represents our lives. The horse represents our minds. Like the rider, we have lost control. We have lost the control to challenge what our minds are telling us. We have allowed our minds to interpret our experiences of life. Because we allow our minds to dictate our experience of life, we often do not feel whole; we feel that something is missing.

Exercise: Mindful Observing

We will not recognize our psychic powers as long as we let our minds determine the course of our lives. To experience our psychic powers, we need to regain control of our horse. It is time to grab the reigns of our minds and take charge.

The following exercise is for practicing mindfulness and to help improve your connection to the natural world. By breaking down the walls that separate you from the natural world, you also increase your connection to the psychic world.

1. Find a comfortable place to sit that offers you a variety of things to look at. It can be indoors or outdoors.
2. Take a deep breath and relax.
3. Spend a few minutes observing your surroundings.
4. Now take stock of yourself by looking inward. Become aware of the thoughts, emotions, or sensations that you are experiencing.
5. When observing, do not judge, evaluate, or analyze anything you are experiencing. Your only job is to be aware of what you are experiencing.
6. Practice this each day, increasing your observation time.
7. When you've finished mindful observing, write down what you experienced and any insights you gained in your journal.

You cannot get this exercise wrong. Even if you catch yourself making a judgment, allow yourself to experience it without judging yourself.

3

PSYCHIC PROTECTION

The Covid-19 epidemic impacted all of our lives on some level. Those who took the virus seriously took precautions by following the recommended guidelines. They wore masks and practiced social distancing. This was especially true for the vulnerable population. Those who were elderly or immunocompromised had to be especially cautious. They could not afford to be infected, as contracting the virus carried a higher risk of hospitalization and perhaps even death.

In a way, being psychic is like being a member of a vulnerable population because we are sensitive to the psychic energies of others. Many people do not believe in psychic powers and many who do have never experienced their own psychic abilities. But as I told you earlier, we all have psychic abilities, though many of us are simply not aware of them. If we are not aware of our psychic powers, we will not experience the psychic energies of others, but will instead believe that the psychic energies we are experiencing are our own. Understanding why some are unaware of their psychic powers requires a deeper look into consciousness.

The Collective Consciousness

Most of us believe consciousness is found somewhere in our heads. From this perspective, we are physical beings that contain consciousness within us. In truth, we are found within consciousness. We live in a universe that is made of consciousness. That which we perceive to be "mind" and 'body" are, in fact, expressions of consciousness that are found within consciousness. In other words, who you perceive yourself to be is actually conscious energy manifested. A wave is both made of the ocean and found within the ocean. Similarly, you are the wave in the ocean of consciousness, and you are also found within that ocean.

There is no individual mind that exists within us. Rather we are accessing thoughts from the collective consciousness. The collective consciousness is the flow of information, known as thoughts, within the conscious system. Every thought that ever existed or will exist is found in the collective consciousness. When we have a thought, we, the manifested expression of consciousness, are tapping into conscious energy.

The collective consciousness contains all information that has ever existed or will ever exist. From the far distant past to the far distant future, information about it is found there. This is possible because consciousness is not bound by the same limitations that we experience as manifested entities. While we experience time and space, consciousness is timeless and boundless. The experience of time and space brings other forms of illusions, including the illusion of separateness.

The Illusion of Separateness

Most of us experience ourselves as a unique and separate entity that exists among other entities. This sense of separateness is created by our ego. Those who become aware of their psychic abilities can do so because they have begun the process of distancing themselves from their sense of ego. This distancing allows them to be more open to receiving thoughts from the collective consciousness.

Most people require continued practice to develop their psychic abilities. Others are born with receptiveness to psychic energy, which was the case with me. However, this ability was hardly a gift, as others like me can attest to.

Most of my life I was bombarded by thoughts that seemed bizarre to me. There were times I felt as if I was going crazy. It was especially difficult in my early years. I was experiencing thoughts that I could not understand, let alone share with others. Because I did not understand what was happening to me, I did my best to ignore the onslaught of thoughts by focusing my attention on playing with my friends or on school.

Over the years, ignoring these thoughts became emotionally draining. I felt zapped of energy and frequently felt depressed.

I believe this is why it took me so long to take my grandmother seriously. It took my grandfather's death to open the flood gates of my pent-up emotions and give myself space to consider the possibility that I was psychic. This is the challenge of psychic abilities. If you experience these abilities but do not understand them, you feel like you are crazy. If you do not experience psychic abilities, you miss out on a large aspect of who you are that can make life deeply fulfilling and meaningful.

Recognizing your psychic abilities creates a greater sense of compassion and a sense of responsibility to help others. You feel you can have an impact on the lives of others through your psychic abilities.

That is why I started this chapter comparing psychic abilities with the Covid epidemic. If you are to guard yourself against becoming infected, you need to adopt protective measures, just as you need to adopt protective measures when it comes to psychic energy. Failure to do so can lead becoming over-whelmed and emotionally drained.

Psychic Protective Measures

There are two reasons to practice psychic protective measures. The more you develop your psychic abilities, the greater your level of awareness will be and therefore the more you need to adopt these protective measures. Obviously, the more aware you are, the easier it is to detect energies.

Because their awareness has not expanded, most people cannot detect the more subtle psychic energies that exist. In a way, consciously developing your psychic skills is like becoming a proficient wine taster, who can detect the subtle qualities of the wine that remain hidden to the untrained palate.

The second reason for protective measures is that some of the psychic energy you take in will have a dark side. The world of psychic energy is full of dark spirits. These dark spirits are nothing supernatural; rather, they are the dark energies generated by others, both living and deceased. Dark energies are generated by those who are identified with their ego. This is in contrast to those who expand their awareness. As awareness expands, the connection with the ego weakens.

Reincarnation is commonly understood as the dead returning in a new form but this is inaccurate. When someone dies, they no longer exist, but their energy continues to exist. It is this energy that can occupy a new form in the next lifetime.

As psychic energy continually exists, those who develop their psychic powers can take in energy from anyone who has ever lived. For this reason, those who plan to develop their psychic powers need to learn to protect themselves. Fortunately, the measures to protect oneself are simple and even enjoyable.

Centering, Shielding, and Grounding

Whenever you become involved with any spiritual work, I recommended that you first follow a routine of centering, shielding, or grounding. This is particularly true if the spiritual work you partake in involves meditation, exercises for intuitive development, and energy healing. When engaged in any of these activities, you are inviting psychic energy to enter you. If you do not have a way to center yourself, these energies can deplete you of your own energy, and could allow the incorporation of dark energy.

Many people on the spiritual path misunderstand the importance of the mind and the body in spiritual development. They believe that the mind and body are inferior and even an obstacle. But the mind and body are invaluable aspects of ourselves that anchor our energetic self to a physical foundation.

Centering, shielding, and grounding all involve some form of visualization and meditation. As I've said, your true nature is neither your mind nor your body. It is consciousness that manifests as a body and mind.

When centering, you are going through the process of anchoring your true nature within your physical body. When grounding, you are strengthening your connection to physical reality. Both centering and grounding are a way to stabilize your energetic self, much like the deep roots of a tree prevent it from being uprooted by a storm. By stabilizing ourselves energetically, we are harmonizing the power of spirit and the body to work together.

There is a balance between the spiritual and the secular as well as the metaphysical and the physical. Centering and grounding give us confidence that we will be protected as we open ourselves to receive the energy flow around us.

While it is important to anchor and ground yourself when dealing with psychic energy, that alone will not protect your dark energy. Shielding is the technique used to guard one against the transference of harmful energies into your energy field. Shielding is especially important for spiritual healers or empaths (people who are very sensitive to the emotional state of others).

Cleansing, also known as energy cleansing, complements centering, grounding, and shielding, with one important difference. Centering and grounding are intended mainly to stabilize your energy field. In contrast, shielding is used to protect you from the negative energy of others. Cleansing is used to purify your energy field. Since you manifested in your current form, your energy field has been impacted by your current and past lives.

We have all accumulated negative psychic energy. It is unavoidable. This negative energy can lead to a lack of happiness and fatigue. By practicing energy cleansing, you can detoxify your energy field and enjoy a feeling of wellbeing, freedom, and a sense of lightness.

Cleansing is also great if you have just ended a relationship, if you are about to relocate to a new area or start down a new career path. It is also useful when you are simply not feeling like yourself.

The following four techniques are going to be used repeatedly throughout the exercises in this book, so you may want to bookmark them.

Technique: White Light Centering

This is a centering technique that we'll use repeatedly throughout this book before doing any more advanced psychic work. Centering is used to connect yourself to your body and is the first step in breaking down the walls of your ego. It will clear your mind so that you will be more open to receiving psychic messages.

1. Get in a comfortable position, relax, and close your eyes.

Pause 3 seconds

2. Take a deep breath.

Pause 3 seconds

3. Hold it.

Pause 3 seconds

4. Now exhale slowly.

Pause 3 seconds

5. Feel yourself becoming more relaxed.

Pause 3 seconds

6. One more time, take a deep breath and hold it.

Pause 3 seconds

7. Now exhale slowly.

Pause 3 seconds

8. Feel yourself becoming more and more relaxed.

Pause 3 seconds

9. In your mind, imagine a ball of white light in the center of your chest. As you visualize the ball of white light, breathe normally.

Pause 3 seconds

10. See the ball of white light growing larger with each breath you take.

Pause 3 seconds

11. Imagine the white light spreading across your upper body and head.

Pause 3 seconds

12. Imagine the white light spreading across your lower body.

Pause 3 seconds

13. See your entire body engulfed in the white light.

Pause 3 seconds

14. Now imagine the white light filling the room you're in.

Pause 3 seconds

15. Visualize the white light engulfing your home.

Pause 3 seconds

16. See the white light illuminating your neighborhood.

Pause 3 seconds

17. Visualize the white light shining on your city.

Pause 3 seconds

18. See the white light shining on your state.

Pause 3 seconds

19. Imagine the white light illuminating the entire country.

Pause 3 seconds

20. Now, visualize the white light lighting up the entire planet.

Pause 3 seconds

21. Finally, imagine the white light shining on the entire universe.

Pause 3 seconds

22. Feel the glory of knowing that all of existence is bathed in the white light that originated from you.

Pause 3 seconds

23. The white light is your connection to all of existence.

Pause 3 seconds

24. Take a deep breath and hold it.

Pause 3 seconds

25. Now exhale slowly.

Pause 3 seconds

26. Open your eyes and feel refreshed and peaceful.

When you're finished, take note of how you feel and record it in your journal.

Technique: Psychic Shielding

Staying safe while interacting with entities on the psychic plane is very important, and this technique will help you do that. It's very similar to the White Light Centering technique, but instead of increasing your psychic connectivity, it uses the white light as a shield so that only positive energies can connect with you.

1. Get in a comfortable position, relax, and close your eyes.

Pause 3 seconds

2. Take a deep breath.

Pause 3 seconds

3. Hold it.

Pause 3 seconds

4. Now exhale slowly.

Pause 3 seconds

5. Feel yourself becoming more relaxed.

Pause 3 seconds

6. One more time, take a deep breath and hold it.

Pause 3 seconds

7. Now exhale slowly.

Pause 3 seconds

8. Feel yourself becoming more and more relaxed.

Pause 3 seconds

9. In your mind, imagine a ball of white light in the center of your chest. As you visualize the ball of white light, breathe normally.

Pause 3 seconds

10. See the ball of white light growing larger with each breath that you take.

Pause 3 seconds

11. Imagine the white light spreading across your upper body and head.

Pause 3 seconds

12. Imagine the white light spreading across your lower body.

Pause 3 seconds

13. See your entire body engulfed in the white light.

Pause 3 seconds

14. This white light is creating a protective shield around you. Imagine that the white light is creating a protective bubble around you.

15. The white light is your protection from any unwelcomed energies.

Pause 3 seconds

16. You can now proceed with your energy work with the confidence that you will remain safe.

Pause 3 seconds

17. Take a deep breath and hold it.

Pause 3 seconds

18. Now exhale slowly.

Pause 3 seconds

19. Open your eyes and feel refreshed and peaceful.

When you've completed the technique, be sure to record in your journal how it made you feel. Did you notice any emotions or thoughts you weren't expecting?

Technique: Grounding

This technique will help you connect to the Earth's energy, which is an excellent way to replenish your own psychic energy while also dispersing any negative energy you may have come across in your psychic work. While centering connects you with your own body, grounding increases your connection to the Earth and the physical world.

Since this is the first technique to connect you psychically to energies outside your own body, it includes the psychic shielding technique from above.

1. Get in a comfortable position, relax, and close your eyes.

Pause 3 seconds

2. Take a deep breath.

Pause 3 seconds

3. Hold it.

Pause 3 seconds

4. Now exhale slowly.

Pause 3 seconds

5. Feel yourself becoming more relaxed.

Pause 3 seconds

6. One more time, take a deep breath and hold it.

Pause 3 seconds

7. Now exhale slowly.

Pause 3 seconds

8. Feel yourself becoming more and more relaxed.

Pause 3 seconds

9. Start off by creating your psychic shield. In your mind, imagine a ball of white light in the center of your chest.

As you visualize the ball of white light, breathe normally.

Pause 3 seconds

10. See the ball of white light growing larger with each breath that you take.

Pause 3 seconds

11. Imagine the white light spreading across your upper body and head.

Pause 3 seconds

12. Imagine the white light spreading across your lower body.

Pause 3 seconds

13. See your entire body engulfed in the white light.

Pause 3 seconds

14. This white light is creating a protective shield around you. Imagine that the white light is creating a protective bubble around you.

Pause 3 seconds

15. Now imagine that the white light of your shield is becoming even brighter.

Pause 3 seconds

16. See the bubble that surrounds you becoming brighter.

Pause 3 seconds

17. Now imagine the white light becoming stronger. See it becomes more solid.

Pause 3 seconds

18. Your shield of white light is so solid that you cannot see through it.

Pause 3 seconds

19. You are fully protected from any dark energies.

Pause 3 seconds

20. Now that you can create your shield of white light, you will recreate your white light shield. When you recreate your shield, do it as quickly as you can.

Pause 3 seconds

21. Now recreate your psychic shield.

Pause 10 seconds

22. Now that you have recreated your psychic shield,

imagine that the energy of your shield is being sent into the Earth. Feel the energy of your body flowing into the ground.

Pause 5 seconds

23. As your energy flows into the ground, feel yourself becoming energized. You and the Earth are joined by your energy.

Pause 5 seconds

24. Feel yourself becoming more and more grounded.

Pause 3 seconds

25. Take a deep breath and hold it.

Pause 3 seconds

26. Now exhale slowly.

Pause 3 seconds

27. Open your eyes and feel refreshed and peaceful.

This is the end of this meditation.

When you are finished with this meditation, record in your journal what you experienced. How did doing this meditation make you feel? This technique takes practice, so repeat it daily. Each time you do it, record your experiences in your journal. Record how the process went for you. Were you able to recreate your energy shield more easily than the day before? By practicing daily, you will reach the point of being able to create your protective shield with only a moment's notice.

Technique: Psychic Cleansing

This technique can be performed any time after you do psychic work. I highly recommended doing it after communing with spirits, astral travel, or being around negative energy. This technique will expel any negative energies you may have come in contact with.

1. Get in a comfortable position, relax, and close your eyes.

Pause 3 seconds

2. Take a deep breath.

Pause 3 seconds

3. Hold it.

Pause 3 seconds

4. Now exhale slowly.

Pause 3 seconds

5. Feel yourself becoming more relaxed.

Pause 3 seconds

6. One more time, take a deep breath and hold it.

Pause 3 seconds

7. Now exhale slowly.

Pause 3 seconds

8. Feel yourself becoming more and more relaxed.

Pause 3 seconds

9. Imagine that you are hiking in the mountains and

come across a beautiful and pristine waterfall. At the bottom of the waterfall is a pool of crystal clear water.

Pause 3 seconds

10. The mountain pool is very inviting, and you walk over to it.

Pause 3 seconds

11. You sit down at the edge of the pond and dip your legs into the cool waters.

Pause 3 seconds

12.You decide to wade into the waters of the clear mountain pool.

Pause 3 seconds

13. See yourself standing in the pool, its waters reaching your waist.

Pause 3 seconds

14. Feel your body become refreshed and energized as the healing waters revitalize you.

Pause 3 seconds

15. You decide to make your way toward the waterfall. With each step, the water becomes deeper, so you decide to swim toward the waterfall. Your entire body is now immersed in the cool, energizing waters of the crystal mountain pool.

Pause 3 seconds

16. As you swim toward the waterfall, feel the rush of energy flow through your body. You are feeling revital-

ized and powerful as the energizing waters cleanse your entire being.

Pause 3 seconds

17. Now see yourself making your way toward the edge of the pool and climbing out of it.

Pause 3 seconds

18. See yourself laying on the banks of the pool and basking in the warmth of the sun's rays.

Pause 3 seconds

19. Take a deep breath and hold it.

Pause 3 seconds

20. Now exhale slowly.

Pause 3 seconds

21. Open your eyes and feel refreshed and peaceful.

When you've completed the technique, be sure to record any thoughts or feelings in your journal.

4

INTUITION AND THE FOUR CLAIRS

In this chapter, we will discuss the four clairs. Clair is a French word that means "clear," and the four clairs are the fundamental building blocks of all psychic powers. However, before we discuss these, it is important that we first discuss another essential concept – your intuition.

Intuition

All of us know what intuition is, and most of us can confidently say that we have experienced it at some point in our lives. Defining intuition is another matter. One of the reasons defining intuition can be difficult is that we often refer to it by other names.

Here are some of the many ways that we refer to intuition:

- I had a hunch...
- I had a gut feeling...
- I listened to my heart...
- I listened to my inner voice...

Examples of intuitive experiences include:

- You had to make a decision, and you had a feeling about which would be the best choice.
- You had a feeling that someone you know was in trouble or needed help, though you had no facts or evidence to back up your feelings.
- When the phone rang, you felt you knew who the caller was.
- Out of nowhere, you had a thought that you should do something or check up on something.
- You get guidance from within as to what to do in a certain situation.

Intuition can be understood as direct knowing or inner knowing. Direct knowing or inner knowing is a knowing that occurs without us thinking about it. If you are deciding on whether to buy item A or item B, you would normally engage in the process of thinking about it. You may think about the price differences between the two items, the differences in their quality, how your choice will impact your budget, and engage in similar lines of thought.

There are other times when you do not even have to decide. Instantly, you know which item to buy. There is no analysis needed in making your decision. Even if your decision makes no logical sense, you know which item is right for you. Of course, intuition can play a role in an infinite number of other situations.

Intuition is a psychic power because it allows us to gain information that our five senses cannot perceive. I remember driving home when I gained information that my wife was upset about something. Other than my intuition, I had no reason to suspect that she was unhappy. I had not spoken to her, nor were there any issues when I had left the house that morning. Further, my intuition came out of the blue. I had not given any thought to my wife's welfare when I was at work that day. Sure enough, when I arrived home, I discovered my wife was indeed unhappy.

A common question has to do with the difference between intuition and thought. How do you know if the information you are getting is from intuition and not from thought? Well, the information from intuition emerges without us having to think about it.

Another way to tell the difference between intuition and thinking involves the element of emotion. When you think about something relevant to you, it is accompanied by an emotion. I may meet someone and have a thought that this person cannot be trusted. With that thought, I may feel concern or fear.

When you tap into your intuition, you will experience it without any emotional entanglement. It will be a pure knowing that is received calmly. In fact, having a calm mind will expand your access to your intuition. This is why we often have an intuitive moment when we are taking a bath, daydreaming, or simply relaxing.

You and I are multidimensional beings, meaning that we occupy different levels of consciousness at any given moment. At our most essential level, we are pure consciousness. Pure consciousness is free of thought. Pure consciousness is unlimited potential, and it is the source of all manifestations, including ourselves. It also contains all the information about the universe.

In our manifested form, we are individuated expressions of pure consciousness. This means that our physical form is a manifestation of pure consciousness. The unlimited potential of pure consciousness has been restricted so that we can experience the world. This restriction of consciousness is necessary, as pure consciousness only experiences oneness. Unlike pure consciousness, which is unlimited in its ability to take in information, we cannot do the same in our manifested forms. The restriction of our awareness is necessary in order to prevent us from becoming overloaded with information.

Intuition is our direct connection to our essential nature. It allows us to tap into the vast storehouse of information that is pure consciousness, which is why it lacks an emotional component. When we experience intuition, we are experiencing the purity of the higher consciousness realms, while the experience of emotions is restricted to our manifested consciousness.

Psychic powers are how intuition communicates to us; they are the channels by which our intuition shares the boundless information of the universe. Those channels are the four clairs. Clairvoyance, for example, is the channel through which intuition communicates information visually. The same is true with clairaudience, clairsentience, and claircognizance. Each of these is a channel by which the intuition communicates information to us, be it through hearing (clairaudience), feeling (clairsentience), or knowing (claircognizance).

Clairvoyance

Also known as Clear Seeing, clairvoyance is the seeing of psychic visions, either subjectively or objectively. When images appear in one's mind, one is seeing subjectively. When one sees something in the environment, this is seeing objectively. With clairvoyance, one can connect with the spirit world through the visions they have in mind or see spirits that have taken on physical form.

Clairaudience

Clairaudience is the "Clear Hearing" of the spirits. As with clairvoyance, this psychic ability involves hearing subjectively or objectively. With clairaudience, you may hear the voice of the spirits in your mind, or you may hear them as though you are having a telephone conversation with them.

Clairsentience

Clairsentience, also known as Clear Sensing, is the ability to feel the energy of the spirit. The feeling of spirit energy can reveal vast information, including things like the deceased's personality, health, and other personal information.

Claircognizance

Claircognizance is also known as Clear Knowing. With this clair, one receives psychic information as insight without knowing its source.

What is Your Psychic Style?

We can utilize all four of the clairs, but most of us have a dominant clair. For example, some people's primary clair is claircognizance. They may receive almost all of their psychic information as insights. Frequently, people will have a secondary clair that they use as well, but not as often as the primary one.

You can think of these abilities like learning modalities. Some students prefer to learn by listening to a lecture, while others prefer to see real-life examples. Still others prefer to actually do what is being taught and others learn best by participating in a discussion about the topic. In each case, the student takes in information using the method that works best for them. As with learning modalities, each of us has our own psychic ability that works best for us.

Exercise: Your Psychic Style

The following is an exercise that you can do to determine which of the four clairs is most dominant in you.

1. Imagine yourself relaxing on a beach. You are sitting in your beach chair and basking in the warmth of the summer sun.
2. As you sit in your beach chair, see the waves rolling into shore and feel the heat of the sun's rays on your skin. Feel the chair under you and the sand between your toes.
3. There are families on the beach who are enjoying their time there. Listen to the sounds of their children talking and laughing. Watch as they run and play.
4. Try to imagine all of these things as vividly as you can.

After doing this exercise, consider the following:

- Were you able to easily visualize images of these things? Were you able to see the waves or the faces of the people around you? If you were, that indicates that you are strong in your clairvoyant abilities.
- Were you able to feel the sand under your feet or the warmth of the sun on your skin? If so, that would indicate that you have clairsentience abilities.
- Were you able to hear the laughing and talking of the children? If so, that demonstrates that you have strong clairaudience abilities.
- Some cannot see images, hear sounds, or feel what they imagine, but they know they are at the imaginary beach. This would be an example of claircognizance.

Another way to identify the kind of psychic abilities you have is through your use of language. The following are examples of this:

- Clairvoyance: "I see what you mean."
- Clairaudience: "I hear what you're saying."
- Clairsentience: "I know what you are saying."
- Claircognizance: "I know what you mean."

For the next few days, pay attention to the words you use. When someone is explaining something to you, pay attention to how you respond to them. Notate in your journal what you say. After a few days, review your journal to see if you can find any patterns in the words that you use. This will help you find additional clues as to which of the clairs is your dominant one. When you find your dominant clair, you can further develop it by doing the upcoming exercises. But first let's examine the four clairs in greater detail.

Clairvoyance

The word clairvoyance is French and translates, as I said earlier, to "Clear Seeing." However, clairvoyance has nothing to do with seeing through the eyes. Rather, it is the intuitive ability to perceive the energy fields around us. Clairvoyance is associated with the chakras of the body.

The word "chakra" is a Sanskrit word, which translates to "wheel." Chakras are the spinning wheels of energy and light. You can imagine a chakra as a whirlpool. A whirlpool is just a configuration of the surrounding water. In the same way, chakras are the spinning wheels of the spirit. The whirlpool is to the water as the chakra is to the spirit.

Chakras make it possible for us to receive information from the spirit world just as the five senses receive information from the environment. The different chakras are found in various parts of the body. Clairvoyance is the information-gathering ability of the 6th chakra, which is located in the center of the forehead and is known as the third eye.

Have you ever experienced a vision that seemed so real to you that you could not stop thinking about it? Or perhaps you had a dream that really left an impression on you and later became reality. Both of these experiences are examples of clairvoyance. In clairvoyance, your intuition is communicating to you through inner visions or even visual perception.

Most clairvoyants access information using inner visions; however, those who can access information using their normal vision can see energy fields and spirits. We all have the potential to be clairvoyants, but to translate that potential into ability requires practice.

Those who are clairvoyant tend to be visually-oriented, experiencing their intuitive powers as images or visions. Here are some examples of what visually-oriented people do:

- When you set a goal, you may visualize its achievement in your mind.
- You frequently dream at night.
- You work in the visual arts, which includes writing or directing.
- You have a talent for remembering landmarks or other visual cues.
- You use phrases such as "I see what you mean" or "Looks good to me."
- You may speak at a rapid rate.

- When you think, others might notice that your eyes move toward the upper left or upper right corners.

If you think you might be clairvoyant, you may want to start a dream journal to record your dreams each night. Then see if they materialize. If you see a pattern, you may be having precognitive dreams.

Clairaudience

Those who are clairaudient experience the spiritual energy around them through hearing. This auditory guidance can manifest as a voice or even music that is beyond the perception of others. That inner voice that we hear, which is the voice of our intuition, is an example of clairaudience. Those with clairaudience have the potential ability to hear those who have passed on, spirit guides, or angels.

Here are some examples of clairaudience characteristics:

- You love listening to those who are close to you.
- You derive great enjoyment listening to the natural world as you attempt to understand it.
- You are an excellent listener and can give solid and concise advice.
- You can channel spirits through automatic writing.

Tip: Create a sacred space for yourself. When you feel overwhelmed by what you are hearing, go to that space. Announce to yourself that you will only allow those beings with loving intentions to enter your space.

Clairsentience

Those with clairsentience experience the spiritual energy around them as feelings. Children are naturally clairsentients as they are tuned in with their feelings.

Here are some examples:

- You have a feeling that something is not right.
- You meet someone, and you instantly feel that they could be trouble and don't trust them.
- You get the feeling someone is watching you.
- You walk into a house and immediately know whether or not it is haunted.
- You instantly know the mood of a room when you enter it.
- You hate clutter and need to keep your living area free of it.
- You take your relationships very seriously, and you tend to be very selective about with whom you enter into a relationship.

Because clairsentients are so in touch with the energy of others, they need to protect themselves from becoming over-stimulated. Clairsentients are extra sensitive individuals, and they can easily be overcome by the emotional energy of others. For this reason, they need to learn grounding techniques or psychic shielding.

Tip: Follow up with your intuition. For example, if you feel that a friend is having a bad day, call them to see if you can verify the accuracy of your feelings.

Claircognizance

Those with claircognizance experience spiritual energy through knowing it. Claircognizants can find themselves in a new situation, with little information to go by, yet they know what to do. This knowing includes a sense of trust and certainty, even though there may be nothing to base it on. Claircognizance is what many experiences as a gut feeling.

Examples of claircognizance include:

- You meet someone for the first time, yet you feel like you have known them forever. You and the other person feel an instant connection with each other.
- You have a gut feeling about what you should do in a situation, even though there is no supporting information to back up that feeling.
- You can make quick decisions.

Claircognizance occurs within the domain of thought. In other words, communication with the spiritual world is experienced as thoughts. This is why many people do not realize they are psychic. Their experience of communicating with the spiritual world is easily mistaken for their own thoughts. It takes practice to discern between thoughts that you have and those being communicated by the spirit world. This is particularly true when it comes to the death of a loved one.

Someone unaware of their psychic powers may believe that their thoughts regarding certain situations are memories. They may believe that they are recalling how the deceased used to think before they passed on. They may not realize that these thoughts could be actual communications from the spirit of the deceased.

These various forms of psychic abilities are how we gather information about both the spirit world and the world of the living. While our mortal lives may be limited, our information flows continuously from lifetime to lifetime. As a child, your life contained information that informed your decision-making and how you perceived yourself and the world. As you got older, that information followed you and continued to shape who you are. Upon death, that information travels into the spirit world and eventually becomes incorporated into your next life.

Understanding Your Dominant Psychic Abilities

In this section you will learn more about your dominant psychic abilities and how to further develop them. We will begin with clairvoyance.

Clairvoyance

When receiving images, it is important to understand these images have significance, even though it may not make any sense to you. Some of the images you receive could be from a time period other than your own. You can receive images from the past, including past lives, or they could be from the future.

Additionally, the visions you receive may be static or they may appear like a movie. If they appear as a movie, the images may seem to have no relation to each other. They may also feel like a dream. Sometimes the images you receive will be symbolic.

As someone who is just starting to learn about their psychic abilities, do not let any of these things bother you. The images you receive may be confusing, but this is normal. As you continue to practice developing your psychic abilities, you will gain greater clarity about the significance of your visions.

You can start developing your clairvoyant abilities by doing the upcoming exercises. Also, use your journal to document whenever you experience a vision. If you do this repeatedly, you will gradually come to understand the meaning behind your visions.

In the beginning, your clairvoyant visions will appear in your dreams. Every morning, record your dreams in your journal. Do this the moment you wake up so you don't forget them. When you journal your dreams and visions, you inform your subconscious that these things are important to you. This will result in you being able to access more information about them.

Recording your dreams also offers the benefit of allowing you to review your dreams in the future. You will also learn to differentiate between normal dreams and prophetic ones.

As your ability to identify clairvoyant dreams improves, you will start experiencing visions in your waking life. These visions will often come to you as flashes, yet they will be recognizable. When your clairvoyant abilities are strong, you will be able to read auras and engage in astral travel. The following exercises will assist you in developing your clairvoyant abilities.

Exercise: Improving Visualization

To improve your clairvoyance, you should work on improving your visualization. By strengthening the part of the mind used in visualizations, you'll also strengthen the part used when receiving psychic images.

1. Take a minute to look around the room you are in.
2. Close your eyes and try to visualize the room, making it as detailed as you can.
3. Try to see the different colors in the room, the different objects, the distance between objects, and so on.
4. Now open your eyes and look at the room again. What did you miss in your visualization? What did you include in your visualization?
5. Next, close your eyes and visualize another room in your house. Take a minute to recreate the room in

your mind. When you are finished, open your eyes and
go to that room.

6. Compare the room to your visualization of it. What
did you get right? What did you get wrong?

Record your findings in your journal. By repeating this exercise
over a period of time, you can refer back to your journal to see
what progress you have made in your visualizations.

Exercise: Basic Precognition with Clairvoyance

You will need either a set of tarot cards, oracle cards, ESP cards,
or playing cards for this exercise. If possible, I recommend a set
of tarot cards. Though oracle cards are better for reading for
psychic beginners, tarot cards are better for this exercise
because each card is connected to many others and that "fuzzi-
ness" is actually helpful for beginners.

Playing cards will also work, but can be more difficult to read
because they are similar to each other. To relax beforehand, I
recommended you perform the White Light Centering Meditation described in Chapter 2 and also concentrate on your breath
for a few minutes.

1. Shuffle the deck, and place one card face down in front
of you.

2. Close your eyes and picture yourself flipping the card
over. What card is revealed?

3. Record your prediction in your journal (this will prevent you from lying to yourself!).

4. Now, flip the card over. Record the result.

Did you get it right? If not, don't get discouraged! See if you were "close." Was it the same suit? Was it the same color card or the same number? If you were using tarot or oracle cards, was the image on this card at all related to the card you predicted? Is the meaning of the card you flipped at all related to the card you predicted (even if it's the opposite)?

1. Repeat for 5 cards, shuffling each time.

2. Over time, look back in your journal to see how you're progressing.

Clairaudience

Unlike the other clairs, it is rare to find someone whose primary ability is clairaudience, since it normally appears as a secondary ability. Clairaudients are sensitive to music and sounds. Sounds that most people find irritating can drive clairaudients crazy.

For those who are beginners, clairaudience is often experienced as ringing or buzzing in the ears. Because of this, people often do not realize that they are picking up psychic energy. As clairaudients develop their abilities, they will start hearing voices. Often, these voices belong to their spirit guides. Strong clairaudients can make fantastic mediums, as they are great receivers of messages from the spirit world.

It is important to note that hearing voices can also be a symptom of schizophrenia. To determine whether you are experiencing clairaudience abilities or you have schizophrenia, ask yourself the following:

1. Do the voices accurately predict the future or give you the information you could not have known in any other manner? Are you able to turn the ability on and off? If so, it's likely clairaudience.
2. Do the voices tell you to do harmful or destructive things? If so, you should immediately seek psychiatric help. There is no shame in this, and you can continue on your psychic awakening after you've received help.

Exercise: Improving Listening

To improve your clairaudience ability, you can begin by improving your listening skills. By training the part of the mind used in listening, you strengthen your psychic listening skills.

1. In a quiet room, turn off the lights and listen to your favorite piece of music.
2. Pay attention to all the individual sounds and see if there are sounds or instruments you've never noticed before.

3. Repeat this for a piece of music you're not familiar with. I've found that classical music works well, including pieces in which many instruments work in harmony.

Record any interesting findings in your journal. As with the other exercises, repeating this exercise and recording in your journal will allow you to look back later and see what progress you have made in your clairaudience abilities.

Clairsentience

Clairsentients experience psychic energy by feeling it, meaning they receive it as an emotion or physical sensation. Clairsentience is often blended with another clair; it is rare to find someone who is only clairsentient. Clairsentients are telepathic and make good energy healers. Energy healers have advanced clairsentient abilities because energy healing requires directing one's energy toward others.

Since clairsentients can easily connect with others, they can receive messages from the minds of others. Empaths are a type of clairsentient who take on the emotions of others. While clairsentients may need to develop their ability, empaths can naturally use their abilities without training, but being born with this ability comes at a cost for empaths.

Unlike clairsentients, empaths are unable to turn off this ability, so they are continuously bombarded by the energy of others.

Further, empaths often have difficulty distinguishing between what they are feeling and the feelings of others. Fortunately, empaths can learn from clairsentience exercises how to gain control of their abilities. The following are some suggestions for clairsentients:

- Practice grounding and psychic shielding daily. This will help relieve you from the emotions you are experiencing.
- If you are feeling an emotional state but cannot understand why you are feeling it, recall the events of your day. Did you encounter someone who could have caused you to feel that way?
- When meeting new people, notice how they make you feel and record it in your journal. Doing this regularly will allow you to look back once you've gotten to know them better to see if your predictions about them were correct. The following exercise will help you develop your clairsentience ability:

Exercise: Feeling the Room

You've probably had the experience of walking into a room and feeling a charge in the air. You may have heard the expression "you could cut the tension with a knife" or may have even experienced something similar yourself. You can get the same kind of feeling between two people with deep but unspoken feelings – as if there's an almost physical connection between them.

That kind of connection between people comes in all kinds of "flavors", and it's important to learn what each means. This exercise will grow your ability to detect these connections.

1. Find a crowded space, such as a store, mall, or library.
2. Before entering the space, try to get a feel for the energy inside. Is it positive or negative? Are the people excited or subdued? Do you detect any specific emotions nearer to you or farther away?
3. Enter the area and look at the people. Based on their outward emotions (smiling faces, how loud they are, etc.), how accurate was your prediction?
4. Record your results in your journal. As with the other exercises, repeating this exercise and recording your results in your journal will allow you to look back later and see what progress you have made in your clairsentience abilities.

Claircognizance

Those who are claircognizant experience psychic energy as insight. This insight can come out of nowhere. I remember driving one day, and I had a sudden insight regarding an area of my life that I had not given much thought to. Before I received the insight, there was nothing in my environment or my thought process related to this area.

Claircognizants are normally curious and intellectual. Unlike the other clairs, claircognizance is difficult to develop, since it involves insight. This means you need to do an exercise that allows you to experience insight before you visualize, hear, or feel the results. It can be done, though. Those who are naturally intuitive can benefit from doing these exercises as well.

Exercise: Forcing a Prediction

This exercise forces you to make a prediction quickly, compelling you to rely on your claircognizance skills. Because it's done so quickly, you're likely to make a poor prediction until you strengthen this skill, so don't give up!

Materials

This exercise requires a pair of dice.

1. Shake the dice and throw them.
2. After you toss the dice but before they touch the table, call out your prediction. The key is to be quick!
3. Record your results. How close were you? Was the number on either of the dice close to what you predicted?
4. Repeat 10 times, recording each result.

Come back to this exercise regularly, each time recording your results in your journal so you can track your progress.

5

CHAKRAS AND YOUR PSYCHIC SELF

B efore launching into this section of the book, I want you to try a simple experiment:

1. Sit down and make yourself comfortable.
2. Now turn your hands so that your palms are facing each other. Keep your hands relaxed.
3. Next, slowly bring your hands together without them touching and then slowly pull them apart. As you pull them apart, make sure your palms remain facing each other.
4. Do you feel anything as you do this? What you should be feeling is your body's energy.
5. If you do not feel anything, keep practicing this exercise until you do.

Your body's energy is not limited to your palms. Your entire body is an energy field, but detecting that energy is easier in some areas of the body than in others. For most people, the palms are one of those areas where energy detection is easily experienced.

Within the body-energy field are energy centers known as chakras. The study of chakras can be traced back to Buddhist and Hindu traditions. The word "chakra" is a Sanskrit word whose English translation means "wheel." Found throughout the body, these "wheels" of energy are located near the major nerve centers of the body and regulate the flow of energy.

The seven main chakras in the body are the root chakra, sacral chakra, solar plexus, heart chakra, throat chakra, third eye chakra, and crown chakra. The seven chakras create a network; hence, they are interconnected. What happens in one chakra can affect all the other chakras.

The seven chakras are continuously changing when it comes to their ability to regulate the flow of energy, much like a car's engine. Fuel enters the engine. Each of the engine's various components interacts with the fuel in a specific way that eventually allows the engine to run. If any of the engine's components are not functioning properly, there will be problems with the car's performance. If not corrected, other engine components can become affected as well.

As you will soon see, each of the seven chakras plays a specialized role in regulating the flow of energy in the body. For example, the root chakra is associated with a sense of stability and security. In contrast, the sacral chakra is associated with creativity and sexuality.

Our physical and emotional sense of well-being depends on whether our chakras are balanced with each other. Besides being associated with various parts of the body, each chakra is associated with a specific element and color. Elements include both earth elements and psychological elements. Additionally, when meditating, color references any given chakra. This will be discussed in a later chapter.

The Seven Chakras

With a basic understanding of the seven chakras, you can learn how to maintain your chakras so that your energy flows properly, which leads to physical and emotional well-being because it raises your vibrational frequency.

The Root Chakra (also known as Muladhara)

The root chakra is:

- Associated with one's sense of emotional stability and security, as well as one's basic needs. When this chakra is open, we feel calm and confident. When blocked, we experience fear, anxiety, or doubt.
- Located near the lower spine.

- Associated with the color red.
- Associated with the Earth element.

The Sacral Chakra (also known as Svadhishthana)

The sacral chakra is:

- Associated with one's sense of creativity, sexuality, and ability to adapt to new situations. When we doubt our creative potential or experience anxiety over any aspect of our sexuality, we create an imbalance in this chakra.
- Located approximately two inches below the navel.
- Associated with the color orange.
- Associated with the element of Water.

The Solar Plexus Chakra (also known as Manipura)

The solar plexus chakra is:

- Associated with one's sense of autonomy, self-esteem, and determination. When balanced, the solar plexus chakra leads to clarity on how to move forward with one's goal. For this reason, this chakra is important if we are to achieve success in our pursuits. Conversely, this chakra can become unbalanced if we focus on our perceived failures in life. Having low self-esteem is caused by the blockage of this chakra.

- Located in the upper abdomen, just below the center of the ribs.
- Associated with the color yellow.
- Associated with the element of Fire.

The Heart Chakra (also known as Anahata)

The heart chakra is associated with our ability to experience love and compassion. It is the most powerful of the energy centers. Emotions are energy forms, and they have a hierarchy as it relates to their vibrational frequency. Fear has the lowest frequency, while love and compassion are on top of the spectrum because they reflect the qualities of our essential nature, which are oneness and wholeness.

The energy of love and compassion dissolves the mind's illusions of separation and our egocentric tendencies. The heart chakra unites the mind, body, and soul, resulting in a sense of inner peace. The heart chakra becomes balanced when the happiness of others becomes our focal point, and we experience compassion and empathy for what they may be going through. There are various popular sayings about love, such as:

- Love conquers all.
- All you need is love.
- Love makes the world go 'round.
- Love is the answer.

These sayings are more than just "feel good" adages. They depict a timeless, though possibly subconscious, understanding of love's power. Love is more than just a sentiment, for its energy is the energy of creation. Love is the substratum for all existence; it is made experiential to us in the form of a feeling.

The illusions of the mind create a sense of separation within us, which creates an ego-centered mind. Fear, a sense of scarcity, and a lack of compassion and empathy are given birth from such a mind. The energy of love dissolves the ego-centered mind. It reminds us of our higher nature, which is the energy of love. If you did nothing else but open your heart chakra, you would regain balance in the remaining energy centers.

What causes the heart chakra to close are any negative perceptions regarding love, be it a failed relationship, the loss of a loved one, or the experience of heartbreak. From the level of everyday consciousness, such events create a sense of pain and loss within us. From the perspective of higher consciousness, pain and loss do not exist, for love is eternal.

The heart chakra is:

- Located in the area of the heart.
- Associated with the color green.
- Associated with the element of Air.

The Throat Chakra (also known as Vishuddha)

The throat chakra provides energy, a passage for energy from the lower body to the head. It is associated with the ability to express ourselves through sound. The voice is our original instrument for communication, predating the written word. More than just sound, the energy from the throat chakra reveals the heart's desires, which speak more loudly than words alone.

This energy center is why the words of others often resonate with us and reach us at the deepest level. The Sanskrit word "Vishuddha" means "pure" or "purification." When we speak with directness and honesty, it is filled with the energy of the throat chakra. When the throat chakra is balanced, one speaks from the heart and is understood by others. The communication of such a one is forthright yet respectful of others.

The throat chakra's imbalance occurs when the ego-based mind attempts to take charge of communication to prove others wrong or prove itself worthy. Anytime the motive of our words is to justify who we are, we have removed ourselves from the throat chakra's energy. When the throat chakra is blocked, we have difficulty communicating what we want to say. We also may believe that others are not interested in what we have to say.

The throat chakra is:

- Located in the throat area.

- Associated with the color blue.
- Associated with the element of Air.

The Third-Eye Chakra (also known as Ajna)

As our level of consciousness rises, we experience things that we did not experience at the lower levels. Phenomena such as intuition, spiritual contemplation, self-reflection, extrasensory perception, and visions of past lives are just a few examples. The potential for us to experience these things has always been there, but we may not have had the awareness to experience them.

The energy center that makes metaphysical experiences possible is the third-eye chakra. The Sanskrit word "Ajna" can be translated as "to perceive or to command." When our third chakra is balanced, we will trust our intuition. Accordingly, we will take action, even when there is nothing to validate the way we feel. Those whose third eye is open are effective as mediums.

When one learns to use the third-eye chakra, one transcends the ego-based mind and can view reality with non-judgment and acceptance. In other words, one becomes a silent witness to all that is. This witnessing is not just of the outer world but the inner world as well. Such a person can observe their thoughts without becoming entangled in them or personalizing them. For this reason, there is clarity of thought. What causes the third-eye chakra to become unbalanced is the doubting of one's intuition due to the influence of others and relying too much on the rational mind. The third-eye chakra is:

- Located in the center of the brow.
- Associated with the color indigo.
- Associated with the element of Light.

The Crown Chakra (also known as Sahasrara)

Along with the heart chakra, the crown chakra is one of the most important energy centers. The crown chakra determines the level of our spiritual alignment. The experience of inner peace, and the ability to communicate with the higher conscious realms, is heavily influenced by the crown chakra. Other spiritual benefits include a deep appreciation for beauty and the feeling of joy.

When the crown chakra is balanced, it serves as a conduit to our highest self. We are multidimensional beings. We simultaneously inhabit the non-phenomenal realm of higher consciousness and the physical dimension of this earthly plane. When the crown chakra is balanced, we are aligned with the higher aspect of ourselves. When it is unbalanced, it leads to self-doubt and a sense of lack of purpose.

The crown chakra is:

- Located on the top of the head.
- Associated with the color violet.

- Associated with the element of Thought.

Exercise: Connecting to Your Chakras

You'll need to get in touch with your chakras on a psychic level before you can start to balance them, which you'll need to do to maximize your psychic skills. This exercise will help you connect to them, so you will start feeling the energies they produce.

In preparation for doing this exercise, I recommend you do the White Light Centering Meditation described in Chapter 2.

1. Close your eyes and clear your mind.
2. Now imagine a red ball rolling across your field of vision. The color red is associated with the root chakra. Feel yourself becoming more stable and confident.
3. Next, imagine an orange ball rolling across your field of vision. The color orange is associated with the sacral chakra. Imagine that the energies of creativity and sexuality are flowing through your body.
4. Imagine a yellow ball rolling across your field of vision. The color yellow is associated with the solar plexus chakra. Imagine that the energies of self-esteem and determination are flowing through your body.
5. Now imagine a green ball rolling across your field of vision. The color green is associated with the heart

chakra. Imagine that the energies of love and compassion are flowing through your body.

6. Imagine a blue ball rolling across your field of vision. The color blue is associated with the throat chakra. Imagine that the energies of the voice and self-expression are flowing through your body.

7. Now, imagine an indigo-colored ball rolling across your field of vision. The color indigo is associated with the third eye chakra. Imagine that the energies of contemplation, self-reflection, and extrasensory perception are flowing through your body.

8. Lastly, imagine a violet-colored ball rolling across your field of vision. The color violet is associated with the crown chakra. Imagine that the energies of inner peace and your higher self are flowing through your body.

9. Now take a deep breath and relax.

Which colored balls were easy for you to visualize? Which colored balls did you have difficulty visualizing? Look back on the association between chakras and colors. If any balls were particularly hard, you might want to work on healing that chakra, which is discussed in the next section. As always, record your results in your journal

When Chakras are Unbalanced

Our emotional and physical well-being is dependent upon our chakras being balanced. Having balanced chakras is important when it comes to developing your psychic power. The following information provides a brief overview of how to balance your chakras.

The Root Chakra (Muladhara)

When the root chakra is over-stimulated, it can lead to issues with the nervous system, including anxiety. The root chakra plays an important role in providing the feeling of security. If you have all your security needs met, the root chakra may be underperforming. This can lead to difficulties in concentrating.

For an over-stimulated root chakra, develop your connection to your spirit through a daily spiritual practice, such as meditation. If your root chakra is underperforming, spend time in nature. You can also do gardening or spend time walking barefoot outdoors.

The Sacral Chakra (Svadhisthana)

When the sacral chakra is over-stimulated, one may overindulge in pleasurable activities. This occurs because we have been resistant to experiencing the full range of emotions. Instead, we have only allowed ourselves to experience things that feel good.

Conversely, not allowing ourselves to enjoy ourselves can lead to an underactive sacral chakra. This condition can lead to low sex drive, a lack of passion or creativity, and depression. If the sacral chakra is over-stimulated, shift your attention to your heart area. Ask yourself whether the activity you feel like doing would be good for your heart and soul. If the sacral chakra is underperforming, engage in activities that bring you happiness and joy.

The Solar Plexus Chakra (Manipura)

The solar plexus chakra becomes over-stimulated when we try to control others. When we try to control others, we are overextending our personal power. Symptoms of an over-stimulated solar plexus chakra include being easily angered, along with a lack of empathy and compassion for others.

The symptoms of an underperforming solar plexus chakra include insecurity, neediness, and being timid. For an over-stimulated solar plexus chakra, try opening your heart to others by showing them compassion and empathy. If your solar plexus chakra is underperforming, start appreciating yourself by taking notice of your special qualities, abilities, or knowledge. Reflect on what makes you special. You can also do affirmations.

The Heart Chakra (Anahata)

When the heart chakra is over-stimulated, we lose our sense of personal boundaries and become a "people pleaser." We strive to make others happy while neglecting our own happiness. When the heart chakra is underperforming, we become cynical of others and feel jaded about love.

For the over-stimulated heart chakra, start practicing self-care by establishing personal boundaries. Show the same amount of love toward yourself that you show to others. For the underperforming heart chakra, extend compassion to others as well as yourself.

The Throat Chakra (Vishuddha)

An over-stimulated throat chakra results from spending too much time and effort trying to get people to listen to us. These efforts are the result of feeling insignificant and invalidated. This may lead us to give up trying to express ourselves and withhold our truth long-term. When this occurs, you will have difficulty expressing your emotions or in articulating how you feel. To balance the throat chakra, learn to speak from a position of integrity. Start expressing how you feel, while speaking in a manner that respects others as well as yourself.

The Third Eye Chakra (Ajna)

The third eye chakra is rarely over-stimulated. Normally, when this chakra is not balanced, it is underperforming. This is a common issue in our society, because we are not taught to honor our intuition. An underperforming heart chakra will lead us to feel cut off from our spiritual experiences.

In those rare cases where the third eye chakra is over-stimulated, get in touch with your body and feelings. Become involved in sports, working out, and spending time in nature. Walking barefoot will also help. For an underperforming third eye chakra, you should meditate and journal about your intuitive experiences.

The Crown Chakra (Sahasrara)

While overstimulation of the third eye chakra is rarely a problem, overstimulation of the crown chakra is never a problem. An underperforming crown chakra is typical of the human species. To raise the functioning of the crown chakra, one needs to balance the remaining six chakras. When this occurs, the crown chakra will be restored to balance.

The following are exercises for connecting and balancing your chakras.

Exercise: Chakra Balancing

If you found during the last exercise that any of your chakras were harder to connect to, this exercise should help. It works by connecting to each chakra individually, and growing the energy of each one as it connects to the next. It ends with the grounding technique described in Chapter 2, to remove any negative energy connected to your chakras.

In preparation for doing this exercise, start by lying down. I recommend lying on the floor if it's not too uncomfortable because lying on your bed could cause you to drift off to sleep. Before beginning this exercise, perform the White Light Centering Meditation as described in Chapter 2.

1. Visualize a ball of warm, red light at the base of your spine. Feel the warmth in your body for a minute before moving on.

2. Next, visualize a ball of orange light just below your navel. Feel the warmth right above your groin.

3. Next, visualize a ball of yellow light just below the center of your ribs.feel the warmth in your upper abdomen.

4. Next, visualize a ball of green light around the area of your heart. Feel the warmth in the area of your heart.

5. Next, visualize a ball of blue light around the area of your throat. Feel the warmth in the area of your throat.

6. Next, visualize a ball of violet light on top of your head. Feel the warmth in the area on top of your head.

7. Now take a deep breath and relax.

8. Finish this exercise by doing the Grounding technique. Do this exercise while still lying down. This will remove any negative energy from your chakras.

How did you feel during the exercise, and how do you feel afterwards? Were you able to feel the energy from each chakra? Record your experiences in your journal.

6

USEFUL TOOLS

I remember when I was learning how to read a book as a child. I was taught to move my finger across the page as I read the sentence out loud. My finger acted as a focal point for my attention. This helped me to focus on the word I was reading instead of getting ahead of myself.

There are all kinds of tools to help you develop your psychic abilities, but it's important to remember that they are simply tools and nothing more. They are like my finger moving across the page. My finger had no part in the reading process; it only acted as a means to direct my attention. In the same way, none of the tools described in this chapter possess psychic powers. Their only purpose is to direct your attention.

The tools discussed in this chapter can help develop your psychic abilities but do not rely on them. You could develop your psychic abilities without ever using them. If they help you, by all means, make use of them, but don't wait to work on your psychic abilities until you have them.

Crystals

Crystals have a long history of assisting people in developing their psychic abilities and in balancing energy. The following crystals are among my favorites.

Crystals for Enhancing Psychic Ability

Amethyst

A powerful spiritual enhancer, amethyst promotes higher consciousness awareness and is also good for healing and protection. This crystal can elevate your vibrational frequency, thus bringing higher levels of awareness of your spiritual nature. The essence of who you are exists beyond the mind and body. Amethyst can facilitate this understanding by expanding your consciousness.

Besides expanding conscious awareness, amethyst will assist you in accessing your angels and spirit guides. Additionally, amethyst behaves like a natural tranquilizer by blocking negative energy. For this reason, amethyst is often used in psychic healing and cleaning.

Clear Quartz

Clear crystals are highly recommended for those who are just beginning to explore their psychic abilities because they offer so many benefits, and are inexpensive to obtain. Great for unblocking negative energy and raising consciousness, clear crystals cleanse and open the body's energy centers. This makes receiving psychic information easier, which can lead to discovering your soul's mission and receiving prophetic dreams.

Iolite

A great crystal for those who are new to psychic exploration, iolite opens and expands one's psychic abilities while offering psychic protection at the same time. Heightening one's conscious awareness facilitates communication with angels, spirits, and other higher-level beings. Iolite is also excellent for meditation, as its energies calm the mind. Iolite is great for keeping you relaxed as you navigate through the different levels of realms of consciousness, and makes it easier to receive psychic communications from the spiritual realm.

Azurite

Azurite works great for clairvoyance and astral travel because of its powerful healing qualities. This crystal can bring about the karmic healing of traumas by healing negative energy patterns. It also dissolves emotional blocks. When the mind is calm, negative energy dissipates, and access to higher realms of consciousness is possible. All of this is a benefit to psychics, mediators, and healers.

Kyanite

A fantastic crystal connecting to the spiritual realm and grounding your energy, kyanite facilitates communicating with higher realms of consciousness. It stimulates the third eye and opens the throat chakra. It also brings heightened awareness to cause and effect. The bottom line, kyanite promotes spiritual maturation and integrity.

Crystals for Psychic Protection

Smoky Quartz

Smokey quartz, known for its ability to absorb negative energy, is a spiritual grounding stone. This crystal is invaluable for receiving and using psychic energy by grounding the spirit and the physical body. In addition, it provides purification and protection to the spirit and body. Because of its grounding power, smoky quartz is also very helpful when meditating.

Pyrite

The strength of pyrite is in its effectiveness as a psychic shield. Pyrite facilitates the integration of high-frequency energy with the physical body. This integration stimulates creative energy, while the auric field is invigorated, and the ability to focus is enhanced. When meditating, pyrite promotes balancing your intuitive and creative impulses with your more practical and grounded state.

Black Tourmaline

As with pyrite, black tourmaline is used for its grounding and protective properties. This crystal promotes focus and dissipates repetitive thought patterns while shielding you from dark emotions. Black tourmaline will ground your spiritual practice in your daily life and will deflect negative energy.

Crystals for Healing

The following crystals are my recommendations for chakra healing and enhancement. However, as a rule of thumb, any crystal that matches the chakra's color that you want to heal or enhance will do. (Note: If possible, find at least one crystal to absorb per chakra and one to enhance per chakra).

Amethyst

Amethyst is an excellent source of healing, and it strengthens psychic abilities. Amethyst is effective for stress relief while enhancing self-calm and inner strength. Amethyst amplifies the third eye and crown chakras. It is very effective for sleep diffi-culties, as well. Just place the crystal under your pillow. Another benefit of amethyst is that it will calm your mind while strengthening your ability to concentrate when you meditate. If all of this is not enough, amethyst also is effective in trans-muting negative psychic energy.

Amber

Amber is known for its ability to absorb negative energy around the solar plexus. It also brings about a sense of stability as well as motivation. A stress reliever, amber promotes compassion and inner peace. It soothes and comforts, especially in times of stress or mental burnout. It is truly a benefit for those looking to experience emotional healing and protection.

Citrine

Popularly known as the abundance stone for its alleged properties for manifesting wealth, citrine facilitates your understanding of the psychic information you obtain. It also offers protection during astral projection. This crystal's healing benefits include balancing chi in the nervous system and clearing auras. An added benefit is that citrine strengthens one's connection with higher consciousness.

Chalcedony

Chalcedony amplifies the throat chakra and heals energy fields. Besides these healing benefits, chalcedony is valuable when performing mediumship or manifestation work. Blue chalcedony facilitates communication when you are involved in telepathic or psychic communication with otherworldly beings.

Fuchsite

Fuchsite is a perfect crystal for healers, as it intensifies the energy of other crystals when combined with them. Fuchsite absorbs negative energy around the heart chakra, and is great in providing protection for empaths. Emerald fuchsite supports psychic cleaning and healing and deepening one's sense of understanding, compassion, and acceptance. It also is beneficial when seeking guidance from your spiritual guides.

Fluorite

Fluorite is valuable in absorbing negative energy around the heart, throat, third eye, and the crown chakras. Because of this, fluorite offers the benefits of increasing mental concentration and absorbing new information.

Garnet

Garnet comes in many colors, with each color benefiting a specific chakra. Red garnets amplify the root chakra, while brown garnet amplifies the sacral chakra and green garnet amplifies the heart chakra. Due to its effects on the body chakras, garnet can activate kundalini energy and bring about enlightenment. Work with kundalini energy, however, must be done with care while engaged in serious yoga practice.

Howlite

Howlite absorbs negative energy from the crown chakra but also restores balance to the third-eye chakra. Additionally, howlite will enhance your visualization abilities, intuitive perceptions, and creativity by aligning you with your higher self. Howlite is also beneficial when connecting with your past lives.

Onyx

Onyx is valuable when engaged in spiritual counseling channeling, tarot card reading, and other energy work that exposes you to psychic influences. It also does a fantastic job of absorbing negative energy from the root chakra. It also strengthens your connection to higher consciousness and taps into the Akashic records.

Rose Quartz

A great crystal for energy workers, rose quartz amplifies the heart charka. It also strengthens the connection between all the chakras of the body, grounding your physical and spiritual being. When this happens, you will enjoy greater alignment with Divine love, kindness, compassion, mercy, and tolerance.

Oracle Cards

Oracle cards are a helpful tool for self-reflection and spiritual insight. They are also simpler to use than tarot cards. Tarot cards are based on a specific system that was adopted from the Rider-Waite deck, originally published in 1909 and considered the most popular tarot deck for tarot reading.

In tarot, there are 78 cards, and each card offers specific insight into a specific situation. There are also specific rules when using tarot cards. Oracle cards have fewer rules, and there is no one way to use the deck, so it offers greater flexibility for the user.

These differences from tarot cards make oracle cards easier to use, especially for the beginner. Also, each deck is designed differently in terms of the number of cards and style. Because of this, you can find the one that resonates with you.

Essential Oils & Incense

Both essential oils and incense provide a scent that aids in enhancing your psychic skills. I recommend that you use them with any psychic work you do. Note: When using any essential oil, read the directions carefully. Many essential oils need to be diluted before being applied to the skin.

Frankincense

This oil has a clean wood-like aroma to it, spiced with fruity tones. Apply it to your skin, and you can add it to your face or body cream as a skin moisturizer and it will provide a feeling of inner peace.

Rosemary

An oil, rosemary has a strong, fresh, camphor-like fragrance to it. It works great for relieving bodily pain such as muscle aches, arthritis and rheumatism. It also offers relief for bronchitis, colds, and the flu. Apply it to the skin. Spiritually, rosemary has a grounding effect.

Sandalwood

With its sweet-woody balsamic fragrance, sandalwood works wonders as a cleanser of negative energy. Sandalwood is widely used during spiritual work. Its fragrance induces relaxation, making it perfect for when meditating.

Sage

The burning of sage to cleanse spaces of negative energy is known as smudging, and is just one way that sage can be used. You can also smudge an object to clear its energy, or you can use sage in aromatherapy.

Patchouli

This oil has an earthy, smoky, and spicy fragrance. Besides enhancing communication with spirits or angels, it works great for treating dry skin, eczema, acne, and dandruff. Apply it directly to the skin.

Myrrh

A resin, myrrh, when burned, offers psychic protection. It was used by the ancient Egyptians for healing and spiritual rituals. Myrrh is effective in clearing negative energy.

Cinnamon

An essential oil, cinnamon will assist in raising your level of consciousness and strengthen your focus. It also is useful for stimulating visions, connecting with spirit guides, and promoting healing and harmony. Use in a ceramic burner.

Using a Pendulum

A divination tool, a pendulum is used in spiritual healing. It is a simple tool, consisting of a string with an object attached to one end. You hold the free end of the string, and the pendulum swings either in a circular or back and forth motion.

Almost any object can be used to make a pendulum, but commonly used objects include crystals, glass, and stones. I recommend using any of the crystals previously mentioned, as well as azurite or lapis lazuli.

Pendulums will respond to the body's chakras, so they are useful tools to detect energy blocks in the body when performing spiritual healing. Pendulums can also be used for clearing energy in the body, aura cleansing, chakra balancing, and grounding. In spiritual work, pendulums provide answers to questions by detecting subtle vibrations from the body. To do this, the pendulum moves in the direction of the source energy.

To use a pendulum to balance chakras, do the following:

1. Suspend the pendulum a few inches over your crown chakra, which is found on the top of your head. Do not swing the pendulum.
2. As you hold the pendulum over your crown chakra, wait for it to move independently.
3. Repeat these steps with the remaining six chakras.
4. Each time the pendulum moves, note the direction it is spinning.
5. Refer to a pendulum chart for an explanation of what the pendulum's movements mean.

Whether you purchase a pendulum or make your own, it is important to know how you respond to it. You want to choose the pendulum that feels right to you. Do this by holding the pendulum in your hands and closing your eyes. Focus on what you are feeling. If you experience a subtle vibration or a temperature change in the pendulum, it will probably be the right one for you.

Exercise: Locating Lost Items

The following exercise involves using a pendulum for developing your psychic abilities. Remember, when using a pendulum, keep your hand still as you hold the string. Do not make the pendulum move. You want the energies of your chakras and the surrounding environment to move the pendulum for you.

Also, before doing this exercise, do the White Light Centering technique.

1. Draw a simple map of your home on a piece of paper.

2. Have a friend hide an item somewhere in your house.

3. Hold your pendulum over the map and ask it to guide you to the lost item. It may start pulling you towards a specific area, or you may have to ask it yes/no questions. Example:

- Is it in this room?
- Is it under the bed?

4. When you ask your question, notice how the pendulum responds. Is it pulling you towards a specific area of your house? If so, try moving into that area and then letting it pull you towards the item.

Be sure to record your results in your journal and see how you progress. Over time you'll learn how the pendulum reacts when it's indicating yes or no, or pulling you towards a certain area. You can make this task harder by having your friend hide something and not telling you what the item is.

Crystal Balls and Scrying Mirrors

Psychics have used crystal balls and scrying mirrors since the 1st century BCE. Unlike the previously mentioned tools, crystal balls and scrying mirrors should be used by those who have advanced their psychic development. They should be used after you have developed your clairvoyance. Scrying mirrors are black polished stones that are used in the same way as a crystal ball. Both of these tools are used to receive prophetic visions.

Candles

Lighting a candle while doing psychic work provides benefits beyond just adding to the atmosphere or providing fragrance. Lighting candles will also increase your focus and inform the spirit world that you engage in psychic work. Candles also affect the energy in the room. White candles will purify the space and absorb negativity. Purple and blue candles support psychic connections, while pink and green candles help connect to divine love.

7

DIVINATION

This chapter on divination is probably the most important one in this book because there is a deeper meaning to divination that is often overlooked. The term divination refers to the ability to gain information about the future or the past. To do this, the tools described in the previous chapter are often used. So, the typical explanation of divination is that someone uses tarot cards, a crystal ball, or a crystal to gain knowledge of a specific period of time. What is frequently misunderstood is that one's ability to use their psychic powers does not require any tools, which brings me to my main point.

We exist in a conscious universe. In other words, the universe is composed of conscious energy. Because we view ourselves as distinct and separate entities, we believe consciousness resides in us. Further, we believe that only living things possess consciousness. Because of the illusions created by our minds and our social indoctrination, we believe that consciousness exists somewhere in our brains. Under this belief, billions of conscious units, which we call humans and animals, roam the planet, going about their day-to-day lives.

We refer to people and other living things as sentient beings. Sentient beings is a term used for conscious beings. Nonsentient beings are those things that are not conscious. Nonsentient beings include rocks, water, crystals, and tarot cards. However, the terms sentient and nonsentient beings are not accurate when viewed from higher consciousness. At higher levels of consciousness, there is only oneness. When viewed from our ordinary level of consciousness, we experience separation, but a deeper look would reveal that everything is connected.

Everything in existence is a manifestation of consciousness, and everything in existence is found within consciousness. Further, everything in existence is permeated with consciousness. Because of this, all of existence is connected to the same consciousness, the one consciousness.

What this means is that rocks, water, crystals, and tarot cards are conscious! They have intelligence! When you use any tool to develop your psychic skills, that tool is just an extension of you. How well that tool works for you is impacted by how you relate to that tool.

Whenever you are engaged with anything in life, be it a crystal, a candle, a dog, or a car, you are engaging with your higher power. This means that you can gain insight into your higher purpose through anything that enters your experience. In this way, anything that you come across in life is a tool for divination.

There are additional more reasons why these tools of divination work. First, they provide a focal point for our attention. Second, a tool can help us achieve our psychic powers when we may not be fully convinced of them. If you were fully aware of your psychic abilities, you would need nothing other than yourself. This is not in any way meant to diminish the value of divination tools, as they can be helpful. But think of them as your training wheels. Once you fully embrace your psychic powers, you can take them off.

The following exercises will help you develop your divination powers. There are many methods for developing your precognitive skills, so find the ones that work best for you.

Exercise: Predicting the Mundane

One of the best ways to strengthen your precognitive abilities is to practice them on mundane tasks. This exercise may seem so ordinary that you may not find it worthwhile, but do not be fooled! In doing this exercise, you are training your subconscious mind to go into predictive mode. Further, it trains your mind to expect that it will be right!

Do the following:

1. Pick a routine task that you do, like brushing your teeth or having lunch.
2. Foresee yourself doing the task before you actually do it. Example:

- Think about yourself brushing your teeth before you actually do it.
- Predict what you are going to have for lunch before you purchase it.

Choose several mundane tasks to predict every single day. Eventually it will become a natural habit, and you'll automatically start predicting less mundane things and see them come true.

The Use of Cards in Divination

The use of cards in divination is referred to as cartomancy. Cartomancy has been around almost as long as playing cards, which first appeared in Europe during the 14th century, when those who used cards to receive precognitive information were known as cartomancers. Tarot cards were invented in Italy during the 15th century, but their use in divination did not occur until the 18th century. Tarot cards became popular in English-speaking countries.

Exercise: Daily Reading

Doing a card reading every day is one of the best ways to develop your psychic activity (and to learn about tarot, if that's the type of card you choose). Much like when starting physical exercise, it may be hard to get into the habit at first, but doing it every single day makes it a part of your routine and means you'll be more likely to stay with it.

A daily reading is also a great way to get into a psychic state of mind at the start of your day, and to learn what different cards mean to you.

1. Every day, after you've meditated, shuffle your oracle or tarot deck and pull out a card.
2. For a minute or so, just look at it. Study not just the image on the front, but look at what's going on in the background. Let the card communicate with you. What messages are you getting from the card? When doing this exercise, keep your mind open and go with the first thought that comes to you.
3. Record your impressions in your journal.
4. Before you go to bed, reflect on what the card indicated about your day, and record your impressions in your journal.

Over time, look back at these records and see if any card that you read predicted an event that occurred after you pulled it.

You'll eventually learn which cards symbolize what kinds of events for you!

Using Scrying in Divination

Scrying is when one gazes into a reflective surface to gain information from distant places or times. The information gained appears as images on the reflective surface or in the mind's eye. Crystal balls and scrying mirrors are usually used for this purpose. If you are able, I recommend that you use a black obsidian mirror. They're smaller than a crystal ball, and I've found that beginners have better results with them. You can find them for under $30, though they're rarely actual obsidian. The material doesn't matter that much.

Cleanse your new scrying mirror to remove any previously attached energy. Glass cleaner is fine for cleaning it. Still, I also recommend burning incense or sage around it, and if possible, letting it sit outside in the moonlight. Sunlight works well too, but it can damage the mirror if it's too bright or hot.

After cleansing the mirror, charge it by burning two candles, one on either side of the mirror, and close your eyes. Envision a white light glowing from your chest. See this light expand and surround the mirror. Mentally dedicate the mirror to the goal of seeing the truth. When first scrying, the images that you receive will usually be cloudy. With continued practice, they will become more detailed.

Also, scrying sessions can take 20-40 minutes, so be sure you are comfortable. If this is your first time, your sessions should be shorter. You can build up your sessions as you become more comfortable with this technique.

Exercise: Starting to Scry

For the following exercise, if you don't have a crystal ball or scrying mirror, a regular mirror will do for now. This exercise is best done in dim light (but not dark). The dimness will help remove most natural reflections, which can be distracting. Before you begin the exercise, do the mirror charging visualization discussed above.

1. With a soft focus, steadily gaze directly into the mirror. As when you meditate, you may lose focus, but simply bring your attention back to the mirror. As you gaze into the mirror, do not have any expectations or judge what you are experiencing. Do not try to obtain a result. Let everything happen as it presents itself.

2. As you gaze into the mirror, relax and continue to breathe. If you feel fatigued, that is OK. Directing your attention is like a physical exercise on the psychic plane; it can drain you quickly until you build up your psychic stamina.

3. As a beginner, do not be disappointed if you do not see anything for the first few sessions. This is normal. When first scrying, it is common to see cloudiness or

pinpricks of light. Continue gazing for as long as you are able.

When you are finished with this exercise, record your results in your journal. Over time, review your scrying journal records and look for patterns that correlate to events in your life.

It is common to not see anything for the first few sessions. I've found it works best after you've started seeing improvements in dream recall and clarity. So if you don't see anything, take a break for a month and focus on your dream journaling.

When you do begin to see things in the mirror, it is likely to be cloudy or merely pinpoints of light. As you progress in your abilities, you may experience:

- Symbols that are meaningful for you.
- Clairaudients may hear sounds that do not make sense.
- Claircognizants may receive flashes of insight without any image.

After you have practiced regularly, you are likely to begin receiving more psychic messages in your dreams.

8

MANIFESTATION

I magine a person going to a magical restaurant. The restaurant has no menu, and the person can order anything they want to eat. All they have to do is imagine what they want and the server will bring it to their table. Now imagine another person goes to this same restaurant but they are unsure about what they want to eat. They have trouble deciding and are also thinking about what they do not want. In this scenario, the server brings every food that this person has thought about: the foods they like, the foods they are unsure of, and those that gross them out.

These two scenarios end differently, and the determining factor is the diner's focus and awareness. The first person focused on what they wanted, while the second focused on whatever thought came to mind. The level of awareness was another deciding factor; awareness of what was being focused on.

Awareness itself is unrestricted, unlimited, unchanging, and constant. What does change is our ability to more clearly perceive the nature of our experience. Imagine if the sun and the moon were thinking beings. The moon may be thinking to itself, "I am the one that creates the light that shines in the evening sky." The moon erroneously believes it is the one that generates light; when it is the sun that is the source of light, while the moon merely reflects the sun's light. We humans are not much different from the moon.

The moon symbolizes our personal consciousness, while the sun represents our greater or universal consciousness. The sun's light is infinitely greater than that which is being reflected by the moon. As long as we believe that we are the "moon," we will have a limited view of reality. However, when we develop the knowing that we are the "sun," we will come to understand that our level of awareness is unlimited, as is our experience of reality.

The Law of Attraction is an inherent aspect of the universe; it is as natural as gravity. Everyone is utilizing the Law of Attraction to create their experience. The only difference between the two people who ate at the magical restaurant was that they understood how to utilize the law while others did not. Further, the Law of Attraction is a testimony to our psychic abilities.

Subconscious and Illusions of Reality

To effectively utilize the Law of Attraction, it is useful to understand consciousness, the mind, and how they create our sense of experience. Most of us have a deep identification with our mind and body. How we experience ourselves and the world around us is informed by our thoughts, five senses, and physical body.

If I am lying on the beach in Hawaii, my thoughts may be telling me something like: "This is so relaxing; the only thing I want to do is enjoy this great beach." Visually, I may be looking at the waves as they travel up the beach, the white sand, the people around me, and the blue sky above. I may be feeling the warmth of the sun and the softness of the sand, I might be hearing the roar of the waves, the voices of other people, and the squawk of sea birds. I might be smelling the fresh and salty sea breeze or the smell of suntan lotion. If I am like most people, I will accept these experiences as real, as they are happening to me.

I feel that experience is happening to me because I see myself as separate from my world. Everything that I experience is in relation to me. If my experience of the world conforms to my expectations and desires, then I feel good about myself. If my experiences are not consistent with my expectations, I may become disappointed and experience self-doubt. Viewed from this perspective, our experience of life shapes our sense of identity. But what if this perspective is inaccurate? What if it is actually the other way around? Could it be that we create our experience?

Because our experience of ourselves is so closely associated with the mind and body, we believe that we are the mind and body. This identification with the mind and body is so strong that our experience of the world, and ourselves, is filtered through them. Our sense of being a physical body creates a sense of separation between us and the rest of life.

Quantum physics has demonstrated that the world of form and physicality is just an illusion, as is the atom. Newtonian physics taught us that all form is made of matter, the basic unit of life. Quantum physics has debunked that belief. Quantum physics has demonstrated that matter is just a myth. The atom, which was once thought to be a solid mass, is now known to be void of any physical structure. The atom is just a fluctuation of energy.

The truth is that, at the quantum level, there is no form. Only at the level of the mind does a sense of separation and physicality exist. Any sense of form or physicality is a projection of our minds, just as we project ourselves into our dreams. At the quantum level, there is only energy and potentiality. At the quantum level, there is no difference between you, this book, and the furniture you are sitting in. What you desire to attract in your life exists there already; you can't be separate from what you desire.

Since everything that exists is just energy, there is no such thing as separation. Everything that you have ever desired, or will desire, already exists within your life at this moment. At the level of normal human awareness, we see that which we desire as being separate from us. Because we feel that we need to obtain what we desire in order to feel complete, our life's energy drops to a lower frequency, preventing what we desire from entering our life. We only attract that which is of like energy.

Energies of the same frequency attract each other, while energies of different frequencies repel each other. To understand the Law of Attraction, we need to understand the quality of the energy we are giving off and how to change its frequency. The Law of Attraction is about frequency management. To understand frequency management, we first need to understand the nature of thoughts and emotions.

Thoughts

Everything exists as energy, and that energy expresses itself as a physical phenomenon. The physical phenomena that most influence our lives are our thoughts and emotions. Our thoughts create our experiences of reality. The meaning of any experience that you will ever have is the product of thought. Your thoughts determine what you focus on, how you evaluate things, the decisions you make, and the actions you take.

Our thoughts also create our experience of reality at even deeper levels. We can illustrate this using a rose. When you look at a rose, it appears red in color, but this is just an illusion. The rose is actually colorless. The light from the sun appears colorless but is, in fact, made of different wavelengths that consist of light from different spectrums: Violet, green, blue, yellow, orange, and red. When sunlight shines on the rose, all light spectrums except the color red are absorbed. It is this color that is reflected off the rose and is detected by your eyes, giving the rose the appearance of being the color red. But the illusion of color is just the beginning of the mind's illusion.

The rose you are looking at is actually found within your mind rather than in the garden. When you look at the rose, or any object, for that matter, your eyes are taking in information. This information is collected by the retina of your eye and converted by the optic nerve into electrical impulses. The optic nerve transmits the electrical impulses to the brain, which then creates a conceptual image of the rose.

Your other senses, such as touch and smell, process information the same way. This information is also transmitted to the brain as electrical impulses. The brain then converts this information and adds it to the image that is created. In truth, all of our experiences are a projection of the mind. Because we see ourselves as separate beings, we interpret these projections as being a physical world that exists independent of ourselves.

Emotions

Our emotions are the equivalent of a car's GPS device. They provide insight into whether we are traveling in the right direction, which is home. What is your home? Your home is becoming aligned with your essential and non-physical self, which is pure consciousness. We are multidimensional beings, with our manifested selves being experienced as the mind and body while our essential self is consciousness.

For consciousness to expand, it needs information, which comes in the form of experiences. Your essential self has manifested as your physical self in order to experience because to have an experience requires a mind and a body.

Having a mind and a physical body creates the belief that we are individual and autonomous beings, which is necessary for creating a sense of separation from the world around us. It is this sense of separation that creates experience, which leads to the expansion of consciousness.

Your emotions are the universe's way of informing you about whether you are aligned with your essential self. When we are aligned with our essential aspect, we experience what we have come to call "positive emotions." When we lose our alignment with our essential aspect, we experience "negative emotions." Any time you feel a sense of love, appreciation, gratitude, compassion, happiness, or forgiveness, you are in alignment. Any time you feel fear, anxiety, anger, envy, jealously, greed, or a sense of lacking, you are out of alignment.

Emotions create a continuum from low frequency to high frequency. At the low end of the continuum is the emotion of helplessness. When we experience this emotion, we feel like a victim and feel powerless to change our situation. Emotions associated with helplessness are despair, grief, sadness, and regret.

Higher on the lower end of the scale is fear. Fear is a higher frequency than helplessness because fear can lead to taking action. The emotion of anger is a higher frequency than fear because anger is more action-oriented. Above anger are emotions such as worry, doubt, and disappointment.

In the middle of the continuum are emotions such as contentment and hopefulness. Further up the scale are emotions like enthusiasm and optimism. Moving toward the high end are the emotions of gratitude, joy, and empowerment. The highest level frequencies are those of appreciation and love.

Before we go any further, it is important to point out that gratitude, a positive emotion, is of a lower frequency than appreciation, making appreciation more powerful for manifesting. This is because the emotion of gratitude is frequently conditional, while appreciation is often non-conditional. We are normally grateful for having received something. I may be grateful for my friends because of what I get from having them in my life. I may be grateful for my health because of what health allows me to do with my life.

Appreciation is non-conditional in that I can appreciate something without gaining anything from it. I can appreciate the goodness of other people for how they help others. I can appreciate a beautiful sunset for its sheer beauty. I can appreciate the dedication that an artist or craftsman gives to their creation.

Our emotions mirror our thoughts. We may not always be aware of our thoughts, especially those that are subconscious, but we know of their presence based on the emotions we experience. If you have negative emotions, then at some level of your being you are having negative thoughts. Conversely, if you have positive emotions, you are experiencing positive thoughts.

By understanding that our emotions are both a mirror to our thoughts and a GPS to our essential self, we can use them to become conscious creators through the Law of Attraction. The key to becoming a conscious creator is to become aware of both our emotions and our intent. To attract what you want, you first need to experience it within yourself.

If your intentions of attracting anything are based on the belief that you need it to feel complete, you will not be successful in obtaining it. Experience what you desire within yourself as though it was already in your life. If you want a relationship, focus on the thoughts and emotions you would have if that person was already in your life.

Exercise: Manifesting Money

Often when people start working on manifesting, they'll start with a vision board and add things like yachts or mansions or fancy cars. But that's like trying to win a marathon when you've never even jogged before. Instead, I recommend people start with something small and obtainable.

In preparation for doing this exercise, do the White Light Centering technique.

1. Get in a comfortable position and close your eyes.
2. Visualize yourself doing one of your daily routines where you are moving from one place to another. Example: See yourself going out for a walk or going to work.
3. As you are moving about, see yourself noticing something on the ground. As you get closer to the object, you see that it is a one-dollar bill. See yourself picking it up.
4. Now experience what it feels like knowing that you successfully attracted this dollar into your life.
5. Record your experiences in your journal and review them later for possible patterns in your practice and what you experience.

Repeat this exercise daily for a week. During this time, do not expect to find exactly a one-dollar bill, as it could manifest in other ways. It could manifest as a few coins or even as a bill of a higher denomination. Rather than actual outcomes, focus on your mindset. With time and practice, you can aim higher and your manifestations will start appearing.

9

TELEPATHY

M uch of the information we have covered so far can be used to better understand telepathy. Telepathy is the ability to communicate with the mind of another through extrasensory abilities. It entails receiving or sending messages through thoughts or feelings, and it can occur over long distances.

The origins of telepathy within the western world can be traced back to the 19th century and the Society of Psychical Research (SPR), located in the United Kingdom. The purpose of SPR was to study paranormal phenomena. Their research was conducted on people who had had experiences that could not be explained by contemporary scientific understanding. Telepathy was classified as extrasensory perception (ESP). Those who had telepathic abilities were tested using a variety of methods, including Zener cards.

Zener cards come with 25 cards to a deck, and each card has one of five symbols. The symbols include a circle, three vertical wavy lines, a hollow square, a plus sign, and a five-pointed star. When testing for ESP, the researcher picks a card from the shuffled deck and asks the research subject to identify the symbol on the card. The test continues until all cards in the deck have been tested.

Researchers have noted different forms of telepathy, including latent, retrocognition, emotive, and super conscious.

Latent telepathy: Latent telepathy is the ability to transfer information, but with a lag time. In other words, an amount of time passes between the time the telepathic message is sent and when it is received.

Retrocognitive telepathy: Also known as precognitive or intuitive, retrocognition involves transmitting information to another individual regarding the state of a person's mind. The information transmitted can involve the past, present, or future.

Emotive telepathy: Also known as remote influence or emotional transfer, this form of telepathy involves transferring kinesthetic sensations by entering altered states.

Superconscious telepathy: This form of telepathy involves the collective as opposed to the individual. In this form of telepathy, the information transmitted involves the collective wisdom and knowledge of the human species.

Given what we learned earlier about the nature of consciousness, it should be no surprise that telepathic abilities exist within all of us. Remember, consciousness is not found within us; rather, we are found in consciousness. We are expressions of the one consciousness, and it permeates all of us. The vast majority of your thoughts were not created by you. Instead, you are attracting thoughts from the Akashic records. The thoughts that you attract are based on the level of your vibrational frequency.

Fundamentally, spirituality is about closing the gap in our alignment with our essential nature, which is consciousness. We increase our ability to tap into our telepathic potential as our spiritual alignment increases. Increased alignment results in raising our frequency. This gives us the ability to attract higher-level thoughts. The greater the gap in our spiritual alignment, the lower will be our vibrational frequency. Accordingly, our ability to access our telepathic abilities diminishes because our lower vibrational level results in increased identification with our mind and body, creating a sense of separateness.

Imagine standing at the corner of a busy intersection and talking to someone on your phone. You cannot hear what the other person is saying because of the noise of the traffic around you. However, when the traffic disappears, you can hear them clearly. This is a metaphor for the relationship between our telepathic abilities and our mental activity. You talking on your cell phone represents your telepathic abilities, while the traffic symbolizes your mental activity, or your thoughts. When your mind is busy with thoughts, and you are identifying with them, you cannot receive the thoughts of others. You are unable to hear them because of the noise going on in your mind! When the traffic of your thoughts slows down, there is space for you to receive the thoughts of others.

Another metaphor we can use is the radio. Before the advent of electronic devices like CD or mpg players, my generation listened to music on the radio. When I turned to the station I wanted, I could listen to music with clear reception. If I was not properly tuned in to the station, the quality of my listening experience was significantly compromised. I would hear static, the music would fade in and out, or interference from other stations could be heard. The strength of the radio signal determined the quality of the sound.

As your higher self, consciousness, you are like a radio tower, while your manifested self is like the radio. To hear the music without static or interference, you need to be on the right station to receive the signal. Not being aligned with your higher self is like not tuning in to the right channel.

The more you take time for self-reflection, the more clarity you will experience when receiving telepathic messages. This is why practicing meditation is one of the best things you can do to strengthen your telepathic abilities. It will also help you develop greater awareness of how you receive telepathic messages based on your primary clair.

Those who are clairvoyant will experience telepathic messages as images in their mind. Clairaudients will hear telepathic messages, which can be both confusing and distracting. Learning to develop your clairaudient abilities can help relieve this. Those who are clairsentient will experience telepathic messages as feelings in their body. Finally, claircognizants will simply have a knowing of what others are thinking.

Most often, our first experience in receiving telepathic messages occurs in our dreams, because we are at a higher vibrational frequency when dreaming, since we lose our identification with the mind and body. By losing our identification with the mind and body, our resistance lowers and we are no longer trying to control things.

When someone you love or have not seen in a while is dreaming simultaneously with you, you can receive telepathic messages from them. This same dynamic can also lead to telepathic messages from those who have crossed over to the other side.

Among all the psychic abilities, telepathy is the skill that most people want to develop. However, telepathy is the most consequential of them all.

From my perspective, telepathy is the most difficult to develop. Very few people ever develop the skill level to be a mind reader, which is a good thing. I say this because being able to read other's minds brings with it an enormous amount of responsibility. After all, the right to the privacy of one's own thoughts is fundamental.

Besides the privacy of others, are you grounded and centered enough to handle the messages you would be receiving? I know psychics who wish they did not have this ability. The messages they receive come with some difficult moral and ethical decisions that they have to make.

Fortunately, most of us will never develop our telepathic skills to this high a level. But developing our telepathic abilities to any degree offers many benefits, and doesn't carry the heavy consequences faced by true mind readers. However, it is still important to protect yourself and others from unintentional consequences, which we will address later.

As I said, we all have telepathic capabilities, but most of us lose touch with them. We become acculturated by societal conditioning that causes us to withdraw our attention from within and direct it outward. By focusing on the world around us, we have become preoccupied with the opinions that others have of us. Our ego-based minds have become obsessed with our self-image. We have developed a sense of separateness and have lost our connection to higher levels of consciousness. This is why children have an easier time trusting their telepathic abilities. They are more likely to trust their instincts.

It should be noted that there is often confusion between telepathy and being an empath. Empathy is knowing what others are feeling, while being telepathic means you can read other people's thoughts. Being telepathic allows you to transmit thoughts to others, while empaths can only receive messages. However, with practice, empaths can develop telepathic abilities.

Signs that you may be telepathic include frequent headaches or sensations in the center area of your forehead, caused by activity of the third-eye chakra. The third-eye chakra is either expanding, or it is picking up telepathic energy. These sensations are harmless, and they will subside as you develop your abilities.

Another sign that you may be telepathic is that you are naturally attracted to spiritual teachings before you develop an understanding of their power. They resonate with your higher self though you may not have yet awakened to your deeper truth. The practice of connecting with your ancestors, the experience of oneness, or exploring your Akashic records are just a few examples of what awaits you when the level of your awareness increases.

Are you good at detecting when someone is lying to you or not telling you the whole story? This is another sign that you may be telepathic. Those who are telepathic can tell when others are not being truthful when they speak.

Have you ever known what another person was thinking without them telling you? Those who are telepathic can pick up the thoughts of others. Those who are clairaudient or claircognizant can do this as well, though they cannot transmit thoughts. Clairaudients will "hear" the thoughts of others while claircognizants will have a knowing of the other person's thoughts.

While telepathy involves receiving and sending messages, it is important to recognize that these abilities are commonly not balanced in any given person. Some people are better at receiving thoughts than they are at sending them and vice versa. When developing your telepathic skills, I recommend that you begin with what you are best at.

One of the best ways to develop your telepathic abilities is to meditate. Meditation teaches you how to focus your mind. Learning to focus your mind will allow you to slow down your mental activity so that you have space to receive telepathic messages.

Exercise: Send and Receive

You'll need a partner for this one, and I strongly recommend you find someone with an interest in psychic phenomena, or at least someone with a playful, willing nature. If you choose someone who isn't interested, they'll naturally block the messages we're trying to send. If it will help, explain this exercise as a game.

Materials needed:

- A deck of tarot or oracle cards. If you have neither,

write down 20 simple words on a piece of paper you can cut up and shuffle like cards.

In this part of the exercise, you will play the role of the sender while your assistant will play the role of the receiver.

1. Sit down at a table with your assistant and make yourself comfortable.
2. Place the deck in the center of the table.
3. When you are ready, pick a card from the deck and examine it.
4. Next, both of you close your eyes.

Instructions for the Sender:

1. Picture in your mind the card that you selected. Imagine it in as much detail as you are able.
2. Now imagine the card floating on the horizon. See it growing bigger and bigger until it fills the sky.
3. Next, think of a word that best describes your card.
4. Visualize the word in your mind. See each letter of the word.
5. Next, see each letter of the word glowing.
6. In your mind, flip the glowing word backward.
7. Now turn the glowing word upside down.
8. Silently to yourself, loudly and repeatedly say the word on the card.

Instructions for the Receiver:

1. Maintain a calm mind; do not hold on to any thought.

2. Let whatever enters your mind appear. Do not judge it or resist it. Do not get caught up with any thoughts that you may have. Remain only as a witness to whatever may appear.

3. When you notice a thought that seems out of place or seems foreign to you, let the sender know about it. When receiving such thoughts, do not judge their significance. There are no right or wrong responses. Just describe what you experience.

4. After the sender has finished, discuss each thought you had. Were any related to the card?

5. Repeat this exercise five times and then switch roles.

Record the results of each card in your journal. Take note of any methods that seemed to help. If you didn't get an exact hit, were the messages received somehow related to what the sender meant to relay? Which seemed more effective, visualizing the card, the related word, or saying the name of the card in your mind? If you don't get any hits after several sessions, consider finding a partner with whom you may be more in tune.

10

ASTRAL PROJECTION

One night remains vivid in my mind, though its memory is less potent now, given that I have a fuller understanding of psychic abilities. I was lying in my bed, trying to get myself in the right state for astral travel. It was my third attempt.

As with the previous attempts, I put myself into a relaxed state while silently repeating to myself, "I am leaving my body now." Soon, I experienced the same things I had on my previous attempts: I felt a powerful energy flow through my body. I heard a buzzing noise that came from within. I felt my body become lighter. But then something happened, and I sunk back down into my mattress.

Rather than being disappointed, I fully accepted the situation without judgment and continued to focus on my feelings of relaxation. I also continued to repeat those words to myself. That was when I experienced something new. The buzzing sound began to sound more like the roar of a jet engine, and my body began to shake violently as my shoulders were pulled up toward my ears. I actually thought I might die, but I fully embraced the moment and accepted whatever may come.

The next thing I knew, I felt like I was without a body. Yet, I was fully aware of what was happening in me and around me. I was moving in ways that were physically impossible before that moment. It was not as if I was flying around or doing gymnastics in my bedroom. In fact, I remained on my bed, but I was bending, twisting, and turning in ways that would be physically impossible under normal circumstances.

Not only were my motions otherworldly, so were the speed and ease with which I was making them. At some point, there was a brief moment during which I lost all memory. When it passed, I found myself peacefully falling asleep. This was my first astral projection experience, but might also be called an Out of Body Experience (OBE). To distinguish between the two, astral travel is experienced because the person has intentionally induced it, while OBE can occur spontaneously.

When astral projecting, people report seeing a golden or silver-colored cord connecting them to their physical bodies. This cord is like an umbilical cord, and it will keep you safe. At any time you want, this umbilical cord can snap you back to your body. I did not experience this cord in my astral projection but it is commonly experienced.

To better understand astral projection, it is first necessary to understand who you are beyond your limited sensory perception. When you look in a mirror, you see yourself as a physical body. However, this perception is illusionary because our sensory abilities, which include the five senses, are limited in their ability to discern our true nature, which is energy.

We are made up of multiple layers of energy, all of which form our chakras and auras. Our outermost energy layer has the lowest vibrational frequency. The limited sensory ability of our eyes perceives this outer energy layer as being a solid physical form. This outer energy layer is created and maintained by the deeper energy layers, which for most of us escapes our attention, as we are so focused on our outer layer.

Collectively, the energy layers below the outer layer are known as the subtle body. These layers have a higher vibrational frequency than the outer layer. During astral projection and OBE, the subtle body moves beyond the outer body in which it is normally found. We can understand this more clearly if we think of the water cycle.

The water is made of a molecule that contains two hydrogen atoms and one oxygen atom. These molecules vibrate because they are made of energy. The further apart the water molecules are, the faster they vibrate. Now imagine the water in a lake. It flows because the molecules are far enough apart that the water moves freely. Imagine the water evaporating under the heat of the sun. What was once a liquid is now gas.

As a gas, the water molecules are even further apart. Because the molecules are so far apart, the gas is formless, colorless, and without any perceivable qualities. Now imagine that the gas molecules condense and form a liquid again (rain) and return to the ground. Because it is wintertime, the molecules move so close together that they cannot move much; they have a low vibrational level. We call this version of the water molecule ice.

The only difference between water as a liquid, gas or solid is the vibrational level of the molecule itself. In the same way, your outer body is like the ice while your subtle body is like the gas. During astral projection or OBE, you are like ice melting and eventually becoming a gas. In fact, most of us do this daily! When we are in deep sleep or dreaming, our subtle body moves beyond its low vibrational exterior. This also occurs at the time of our death.

Everything that we experience in our everyday consciousness belongs to the lower realm that we normally inhabit. But astral projection provides amazing opportunities for exploring higher realms of consciousness. No longer restrained by physical limitations or the limitations of the rational mind, you can fly, pass through solid objects, or explore distant places. Astral traveling allows you to travel across the different realms of consciousness.

By entering higher realms, you experience a whole new reality where the rules of the lower realm do not apply. You can receive visions of the past or the future or access the Akashic records. Time and space do not exist in the higher realms. Some believe that our dreams are actually enacted at these higher realms of consciousness. This means that when you have a dream, your astral self is actually observing its enactment at higher realms of consciousness. This is why lucid dreaming has a strong connection to astral projection. Most profoundly, you gain a greater understanding of your essential nature, since you are actually experiencing it!

The ability to astral project obviously takes time and requires further development of your psychic abilities, as well as a great deal of patience. Those who have developed strong clairvoyant abilities are most likely to be successful in this ability.

The experience of astral projection can be emotionally over-whelming, which can cause you to return to your body. This is common for beginners, which is why it takes repeated practice before you accept these experiences. It is helpful to remember that astral projection is safe and that you are always in full control. You can return to your body anytime you want, and it happens instantaneously. Any fears you experience are the products of your rational mind, which cannot conceive of what is being experienced.

Another thing to keep in mind is that you do not just automati-cally end up at your desired destination when astral traveling.

Astral travel is just like physical travel, in that you need to be intentional. Before you leave your physical body, you need to know where you want to go. When you leave your body, you need to take action to get to where you want to be. You can do this by walking, flying, or teleporting. When first starting, I recommend that you walk, as the other modes of traveling can be too shocking for a beginner. With practice, you can progress to flying or teleporting.

When teleporting, imagine that there is a door behind you. When you turn around, you'll see the door, and you can open it and step through to wherever you want to go. When you want to return to your body, you simply have to think about doing so. If that doesn't work as quickly as you'd like, float upwards and then let yourself fall. This always snaps me right back to my body. The following are exercises for astral traveling:

Exercise: Dream Travel

Traveling in your dreams is much easier than when awake, so it's a good place to start. To succeed, I recommend practicing this exercise every night. Don't be surprised if this one takes a while to achieve, as dreams are difficult things to grab control of, and don't attempt this until you have developed strong dream recall ability due to a well-maintained dream journal.

1. Before going to bed, set a strong intention in your mind to travel to a specific place. For a beginner, I highly recommend taking short trips - to your place of

work, a friend's house, or anywhere nearby that you enjoy visiting. This will help with the emotional "shock" of arriving where you intended.

2. You can set your intention by repeating in your head, "I will travel to_____ in my sleep." As you drift off to sleep, try to keep the intention fixed in your mind.

3. As your mind prepares for astral travel, you may experience tingling in your body, strange visions, or a high-pitched whine. These experiences can be disconcerting, but it's just your spirit preparing to separate from your body and travel.

When you awaken, record your results in your dream journal. Did you arrive at the place you intended, or did you travel somewhere else? Did you see the silvery cord connecting you to your body?

Exercise: Astral Travel

Attempting this exercise before success in dream travel is likely to lead to frustration. You can perform this with your eyes closed, as if meditating, or you can use your scrying mirror. For beginners, I don't recommend setting a firm intention of a destination. Instead, just go wherever your spirit leads you.

1. Begin by visualizing as vividly as you can your body as it is right now.
2. Slow your breathing.

3. Visualize your spirit standing up and leaving your body. You will feel a warmth or tingling sensation, and it may be difficult to get your spirit to exit your body. Once you do leave your body, you may "snap back" out of excitement. If so, go ahead and open your eyes and consider the exercise a success!

4. See the astral thread that connects your spirit to your body, and know that you are always safe because of it.

5. Start by walking around the room. Look with your eyes at the room you're in. Move to each corner of the room and turn to look at your body, still seated in meditation.

6. Return to your body and visualize your spirit reentering your body.

7. Open your eyes.

Record your results in your journal. Which part of the exercise was hard and which was successful? Once you've been able to completely move around the room you're in without snapping back to your body, you can try floating in your room and then traveling outside your home.

11

READING AURAS

I n Chapter 10, as we learned about astral projection, we also learned that the body consists of multiple layers of energy. Those layers below the outer layer, which we experience as our physical body, are collectively referred to as the subtle body. These energy layers create energy fields that extend beyond the body. These energy fields are called auras. They can provide important information about our physical and spiritual health.

While most people have heard of auras, they would probably tell you that they cannot be seen. Yet, this claim is only valid at the conscious level of their awareness. Those at higher levels of awareness most likely have seen auras but simply do not realize it. A clue to this unrecognized awareness is found in the expressions that we commonly use. How often have we heard things like:

- He is green with envy.
- She is feeling blue.
- He has a good vibe about him.
- There is something dark about him.
- She is seeing red.

These are just some of the common expressions we use that reflect our ability to detect auras, though it's happening at a subconscious level. Children, however, are different. They tend to be aware of auras, but do not understand their meaning or their significance. This is why children frequently color people green or blue. Because of our social indoctrination to shift our attention away from within, we lose our ability to detect auras as we get older.

The study of auras can be traced back to Hinduism and Indian theosophy. However, the concept was made popular by a priest named Charles Webster Leadbeater in 1910. Leadbeater introduced the topic of auras by incorporating it into his studies of chakras. Later, others in the theosophist movement also adopted the concept of auras. But auras did not gain widespread popularity until the 1980s, when they became part of the New Age movement. By this time, the original Hindu and Indian roots of auras had been forgotten.

The Seven Layers of Energy

Let's return to our different layers of energy. Each of these layers is associated with a specific chakra in the body. It is these layers of energy that we experience when we see auras. The following is a description of the different layers.

The Etheric Layer: The Etheric is the first layer of our energy field, and is the closest one to the body. Of all the layers, it has the slowest vibrational frequency. This layer is associated with the root, or base chakra, and it reveals information regarding physical health.

The Emotional Layer: The second layer, the emotional layer, is found above the etheric layer. It has a higher vibrational frequency than the etheric layer, which determines our emotional experience.

The Mental Layer: The third layer, the mental layer, is found above the emotional layer, and has a higher vibrational frequency than the emotional layer. The mental layer is the source of our mental activity, including our thoughts, judgments, self-control, and other mental functions. It is associated with the solar plexus chakra.

The Astral Layer: The astral layer acts to join the lower vibrational energies of the physical plane with the higher frequency energies of the spiritual plane. This fourth layer is associated with the heart chakra.

The Etheric Template: Located above the astral layer, the etheric template has a higher vibrational frequency than the astral layer. It creates our experience of the physical body. It is the creative energy of this layer that causes the formless to eventually become form.

The Celestial Layer: This sixth layer is found above the etheric template, and it also has a higher vibrational frequency. This layer is associated with the third-eye chakra. It is where spiritual development begins, as well as the stages that lead to enlightenment. It is also where perception takes place.

The Ketheric Layer: This seventh layer is the portal to divinity and higher consciousness. This layer has the highest vibrational frequency of all the layers and is associated with the crown chakra.

We can only see the auras of the first five layers, since the vibrational frequency of the 6th and 7th layers are too high for our eyes to detect. Those who can connect to their psychic mind will see the colors of the first five layers. We all have the potential to do so.

The Colors of Wellness

The colors of a person's auras provide valuable information about their physical, mental, and spiritual well-being. The following is a description of what the different colors of auras mean:

Red: The color red is a sign of courage, strength, and energy.

Brick red: A brick red aura indicates angry or dark energies.

Deep red: Auras that have a deep red color indicate the energy of sensuality.

Crimson: The color crimson indicates loyalty.

Pink: Pink-colored auras signify optimism and cheerfulness.

Rose: Auras that are rose-colored indicate self-love.

Orange: The color orange indicates that the person is balanced mentally and physically and is vital and joyous.

Yellow: Yellow-colored auras signify wisdom and creativity as well as spiritual openness.

Grayish yellow: A grayish-yellow color indicates fearful thoughts.

Green: A green-colored aura indicates growth, compassion, and ingenuity.

Pale green: Pale green signifies healing.

Grayish green: A grayish-green aura indicates envy or pessimism.

Blue: A blue-colored aura means that the person possesses idealism, intellectual power, imagination, and spiritual understanding.

Grayish blue: A grayish-blue indicates a state of melancholy.

Ice blue: An ice-blue colored aura indicates the person is an intellectual.

Purple: A purple aura is a sign of spiritual power.

Each aura is unique in its size, color, or shape. Further, auras change as the person's mental and physical state changes. Additionally, each psychic perceives auras differently in the same way that each person is impacted by a work of art differently. Some will notice fine details, while others will merely notice the overall image.

When you view auras for the first time, they will likely appear colorless and hazy. The more you develop your psychic abilities, the more details you will notice when perceiving auras. You will begin to see their colors.

Also in the beginning, you will probably see auras randomly, meaning that you will not see the aura of every person. This, too, will change with practice as your ability to see auras will occur more frequently. Those who are in a strong emotional state will be the easiest for you to spot.

The intensity of a person's aura is a sign of how spiritually developed they are. Most people will have a light aura, while those who have developed their spiritual gifts will be denser and more vivid.

Exercise: Seeing Your Own Aura

Seeing your own aura is easier than seeing those of other people because you can choose the right location and timing, and you can force yourself to sit still to concentrate. For beginners, seeing the auras of others can be difficult due to the environment. This exercise is best performed in a slightly dim room. Prepare for the exercise by performing the White Light Centering Meditation from Chapter 2.

Materials needed:

1 white sheet of paper (optional)

1. Sit in a comfortable position and relax.
2. Place the white sheet of paper on a flat surface.
3. Next, place your hands in front of you and turn your elbows outward so that your hands are pointing at each other and are directly above the white paper. The sides of your hands should be parallel with the front of your body.
4. With your forefingers extended, bring your hands toward each other until the tips of the forefinger of each hand touch.
5. Watch them for about 10 seconds, and then slowly move them apart. Focus on the white paper beneath your hands instead of the hands themselves.
6. You'll notice a thin line of almost invisible energy connecting them, which will break as they move apart. Note: This breakage will happen quickly for beginners, but as you develop your abilities, the link will stay attached longer.
7. When you can see the link extend for at least a half-

inch, you can modify the exercise by touching all four fingers of both hands together and then withdrawing them.

8. You may be disappointed that your own aura is almost colorless and thin, but don't worry. As you grow in this practice, you'll start to see the colors.

Remember to record the results in your psychic journal. Did you see your aura when using your forefingers, or all your fingers? Did you notice any color?

Exercise: Seeing Other People's Auras

After you've been able to see your own aura, you'll know better what to look for and what to expect from others, so you can ask for a partner to help out with the following exercise. As with the telepathy exercise, it helps to find someone with a curious and open attitude.

1. Ask your partner to stand in front of a plain colored wall.
2. Stand back several feet and look towards your partner. Focus on the wall behind them.
3. Let your eyes become unfocused and remain in a relaxed state.
4. It may take several minutes, but you'll become aware of a haze around your friend. It may be concentrated only around their head and neck.

5. When you see the aura, try focusing on it. It may disappear the first few times you try it.

6. When you can see the aura continuously for several seconds, ask your partner to think of their happiest memory. See if you can detect any color shift in their aura.

Record your results in your psychic journal. Were you able to see any color in the aura? Did the color match what you were expecting to see? Was the aura thick or thin?

Exercise: Seeing Aura Colors

Many people can see the misty outlines of auras without much effort. Still, some get stuck there and are unable to see the aura colors. This exercise will help.

1. Choose a person whose aura you want to see. It helps to choose someone you see often and have a positive relationship with.

2. For a week or so, make a note of what colors that person chooses to wear. Often people subconsciously choose colors to wear that match their auras, so it may give you a hint of what to look for.

3. Sit down at a table with a piece of paper and some colored markers. If you don't have markers, you can use crayons or colored pencils, but I've found that the vibrant colors of markers work best.

4. Close your eyes and visualize the person as vividly as you can. Based on what you've learned about aura colors, ask yourself what color you'd expect to see in their aura. Picture in your mind the aura radiating off the person.

5. Now open your eyes and draw the person as well as you can. Artistic talent isn't required. If a stick figure is the best you can do, go for it. Be sure to color in their clothing and their aura as you imagined it.

Repeat this exercise several times over the next week, and then try the previous exercise with them again.

12

MEDIUMSHIP & SPIRIT GUIDES

Those who develop their psychic skills can receive guidance from the ancient wisdom that exists both on our physical plane and from the afterlife. This guidance can come from those who have entered the afterlife as well as from spirit guides.

Mediums & Mediumship

Mediums have developed psychic abilities to communicate with those who have passed on to the spirit world. They are the go-between for the afterlife and the world of the living. They tell us what the spirit world has to say while at the same time communicate to the spirit world what we ask. In this manner, mediums are like a three-way communication channel. The spirit world communicates to the medium while the medium communicates to the recipient, a loved one, or interested parties.

How mediums communicate with spirits varies from medium to medium. There is a range of abilities they can use. Just as we explained psychic styles in Chapter 4, think of these abilities as being like learning modalities. Some people prefer to learn by listening to a lecture, while others prefer to see real-life examples. Still others prefer to actually do what is being taught while others learn best by participating in a discussion about the topic.

As with learning modalities, mediums use the abilities that work best for them, which can be in the form of clairvoyance, clairaudience, or clairsentience.

The Two Kinds of Mediumship

There are two major kinds of mediumships: mental mediumship and physical mediumship. The type of powers that mediums use to communicate with the spirit world determine which kind of mediumship they are using. Each mediumships has its own way in which they communicate with the spirit world. Mental mediumship involves communicating with the spirit world through their mind. In contrast, physical mediums communicate with the spirit world through the manifestation of phenomena. The following is an overview of both.

Mental Mediumship

Mental mediums, commonly known as psychic mediums, receive information from the afterlife through their mental functions. In other words, when the deceased's spirit communicates with the medium, the information received is experienced as images, visions, verbal messages, and energies. In turn, the medium communicates the message to those who are in attendance. Mental mediums can receive a wide range of factual information from the deceased, such as names, location information, and information about their death. The accuracy of the information is determined by the attendees of the session.

Physical Mediumship

While mental mediums communicate with the spirit world through mental activity, physical mediums receive information from the afterlife in physical experiences. A physical medium will pick up sensory information from the deceased, such as odors, feelings, sights, or sounds. The physical medium will often go into a trance to receive this information, which allows them to be more receptive to this kind of information.

As I've said many times throughout this book, we all have psychic abilities, though we may not be aware of them. Because of this, we all have the potential to become mental mediums. However, only a few have the potential to become physical mediums. To be a physical medium, one needs to be born with certain aspects, which have yet to be identified.

Physical mediumship involves allowing the spirit to temporarily take over one's body. For this reason, the medium must be sensitive and receptive enough to the spirit's willingness to do so. But possessing such a level of sensitivity means that this person will have a more difficult time dealing with daily life. This is why physical mediumship is so rarely found today.

Developing Mediumship Abilities

For those who wish to develop their mediumship abilities, it is important to remember that you should first develop your other psychic abilities discussed throughout this book. This is especially true of meditation and dream recall. Meditation will allow you to quiet your mind and become centered, which will help you to be more sensitive to information from higher levels of consciousness, which is the realm of those who passed away. Developing your dream recall is important because dreams provide the easiest access to the afterlife, especially for beginners.

For beginners, I recommend that you start developing your mediumship abilities by selecting a loved one who has passed who you most want to hear from. Find photographs of them and place them around your home. Take time each day to talk to these pictures. Talk out loud as though you were having a conversation with them. You can tell them about your day and let them know that you miss them and that you want to hear from them. By doing this, you are informing the spirit world that you want to hear from them.

Once you have done this, go on with your day but stay alert to any signs that your loved one may be sending you. They will often communicate with you in a way that you can detect with your senses. This would include the following:

- Flashes of light and color in the periphery of your vision.
- Tingling sensations in your body.
- Sudden odd smells.
- Subtle shifts in energy.

Communicating with those other than your loved ones can be more challenging, as they are more difficult to control. These spirits can act like children who are seeking attention. For these kinds of spirits, it is recommended that you set firm boundaries with them. For example, you can tell them that you will only communicate with them during a specific time of the day. If they do not respect your boundaries, ignore them.

Exercise: Dream Mediumship

As with many psychic abilities, mediumship is easier in dreams before moving to the waking world. When we're asleep, we're more connected to our subconscious mind, and thus to the psychic plane. In this exercise, you'll work to establish contact with someone near and dear to you, because they're more likely to hear you calling to them, and more likely to want to help.

1. Choose a deceased loved one who has passed on to the other side with whom you'd like to communicate.

2. Decide on a series of questions you'd like to ask them or things you'd like to tell them. Write them down in your psychic journal before going to bed.

3. As you drift off to sleep, ask them to visit you in your dreams. Repeat the request in your head while visualizing them as best you can as you last remembered them. It will help to hear their voice in your head, and remember the sensation of touching them.

When you wake in the morning, record your results in your journal. Did you establish contact? If not, did you dream of being in a place you remember being with them? Did you hear any voices, or was there anything else in your dream that reminded you of them? It will help to repeat this process a few times a week.

Spirit Guides

The concept of spirit guides has been around since ancient civilizations. Even before the expansion of Christianity and Islam, spirit guides were deeply entrenched in traditional African culture. To this day, many Africans believe that the spirits of their ancestors live on eternally, providing them with guidance and protection. Spirit guides are seen as the go-betweens of the living and God.

In Western culture, spirit guides are not necessarily the descendants of humans, as there are numerous other spiritual types.

Some spirit guides exist as energy or light beings and inhabit the cosmic domain, having never inhabited our earthly plane. From a Western perspective, spirit guides are energetic beings who have fulfilled their life purpose and have taken on the role of a protector or guide to the living. The following are descriptions of the more common spirit guides.

Guardian Angels and Life Guides

Each one of us has a guardian angel that has opted to serve us. Guardian angels assist us by helping us accomplish our life's purpose. These spirit guides have a high vibrational frequency; hence, their dominant quality is unconditional love. Their high vibrational frequency enables them to provide us with wisdom and knowledge when needed.

Since the vibrational level of our guardian angel is higher than our own, it causes ours to rise. This increase in our vibrational level allows us to receive their knowledge and wisdom. Unlike other kinds of spirit guides, guardian angels are always with us.

Life guides play more of an organizational role. They coordinate all the other spirit guides so that the right ones are always available to ensure that your life does not get too crazy. An important thing to remember with life guides, as with all guides, is that you need to be open to receive their messages. As powerful as they may be, they cannot supersede your free will. If we are not receptive to their guidance, we can become overwhelmed by our lives.

Divine Timing Guides

We may believe that we are free-willed beings who can choose freely and shape our own destiny. This perception is warranted, given the level of our conscious awareness. However, at higher levels of consciousness, everything that we hold true falls apart. Such a realm of consciousness is where the divine timing guides reside.

These spirit guides are the ones that possess the master plan of our lives. Unbeknownst to us, everything that we experience was predestined. Divine timing guides are the ones in charge of seeing that everything that happens in your life happens at the right time. Divine timing guides also are the ones behind our experience of synchronicity. It is important to note that you and I are not separate entities from the divine timing guides, or any other guide, for that matter.

Once again, at our most essential level, we are pure consciousness. How we experience ourselves is the physical manifestation of pure consciousness. We are multidimensional beings who are simultaneously conscious beings and consciousness itself. This means that the concept of free will and the concept of having our lives preplanned are not two incompatible realities.

Creative Guides

If you ask an artist, a musician, or a writer where they get their creative ideas, many will tell you that they just come to them. The artist will tell you they just had a 'knowing' about how to approach their artwork. The musician will say that their music came through them, and the writer will similarly say that the words simply starting flowing.

In all of these cases, the person's artistic endeavors came largely from the guidance of their creative guides. These artistic individuals were open to receiving the creative energy provided by these guides. Creative guides do not only serve artists. They can serve each of us if we are willing to be open to their guidance. Creative guides are available to us for problem-solving or decision-making. They can get us to view life through a new perspective that provides us opportunities to come up with answers beyond the realm of ordinary thinking.

Teacher Guides

Teacher guides offer lessons that will keep us from straying from our path. Each of us follows a path that will lead to our understanding of our life's purpose. The experiences we have each day are all created by the spirit world to guide us to a deeper understanding of our essential truth and reality itself.

When we awaken to these truths, we will be liberated from the sufferings that come with the belief that we are a limited and separate self. This journey of self-discovery that the teacher guides provide us with are the lessons that will keep us on the path that is correct for us. The lessons that teacher guides provide can be found in our dreams, meditations, or can even be subtle signs that we encounter in everyday life.

At the most fundamental level, the teacher guides are our experiences, both good and bad. It is important to remember that "good" and "bad" are the exclusive products of the mind. There is nothing in life that is inherently good or bad. We simply form judgments and impose them on our experiences. In this manner, life is a continuous feedback loop that informs us whether we are moving forward on our path or if we have lost our way.

Spirit Animal Guides

Spirit animal guides are ascended beings who offer us guidance, protection, and assistance. They are deeply grounded in nature, and their mission is to guide us in keeping our energy grounded as well. From the Native American perspective, spirit animals are the manifestation of a spiritual guide. The spirit animal guide that enters our lives possesses qualities that mirror our own, but which may be latent within us. In this way, our spirit animal is reminding us of what we already possess. If we took advantage of these qualities, we would experience life with greater ease, enjoyment, and success.

Spirit animal guides are an important part of the Native American belief system. They believe that spirit animals come to us during times of great change. They guide us through times of uncertainty by teaching us the wisdom of their species. For example, if the spirit animal is a wolf, it would teach us the wisdom of the wolf.

Spirit animals do not teach using words. Instead, it is up to us to discern the wisdom of the animal in how it survives. Spirit animal guides can appear in our dreams or meditations. Each person has their own spirit animal.

Exercise: Communicating with Spirits Using Automatic Writing

Automatic writing is the process of letting a spirit into your body to control your hand while you write. Because you're inviting a spirit into your body, it's important to protect yourself beforehand, so we'll be using the Psychic Shielding technique. The exercise is best performed in a dimly lit room. Also, I recommend you light a white candle to announce your intentions to the universe and also set any helpful crystals on the table you're working at.

Materials needed:

- Piece of paper
- A pen or pencil (a pen is recommended, as it requires less pressure when writing)

1. Sit down in a relaxed position that makes it easy for you to write.
2. Write your question at the top of the piece of paper in your journal. If you don't have a specific question, ask for guidance.
3. Close your eyes.

4. Begin with a White Light Centering and Psychic Shield (see Chapter 3).

5. Visualize the energy around you flowing into your writing arm. Feel the warmth in your arm.

6. Open your eyes with a soft focus on the paper.

7. Begin writing. Do not stop to think about what to write. Instead, trust the process and let the writing flow through you. Begin with any impressions you have, and then write any random thought that comes to mind. It's important to just start writing, even if you have no idea where you're heading. The act itself should help trigger messages from the spirit world.

Once you've finished, perform a Grounding Meditation from Chapter 3, just in case you came in contact with any negative energy or entities. When done, look back over what you wrote, and record any thoughts in your journal.

Exercise: Meeting Your Spirit Guide

Meeting your spirit guide is a huge step for a psychic, as they can aid you with many tasks in the psychic world and keep you safe as well.

1. Start with a meditation of at least 20 minutes, and then perform the White Light Centering Technique.

2. With your eyes closed, ask your spirit guide to show themselves to you in your mind's eye.

3. You should start to see shapes in your mind's eye. They will often be hard to focus on and may disappear quickly.

4. As you experience these shapes, create a feeling of love and warmth in you to help the shapes stabilize.

For each session, record your results in your journal. With practice, you will be able to watch the shapes coalesce into a coherent shape that your spirit guide has chosen to manifest. You'll eventually be able to communicate with your spirit guide as well, though the form of that communication may vary depending on your natural psychic skills.

CONCLUSION

Have you ever seen a baby learn to walk? They repeatedly attempt to walk, though the beginning can be rough going. There are plenty of falls, but the encouragement they receive from their parents helps them to keep trying. Before learning to walk, babies have no concept of walking, because it had not been part of their experience.

The question is what is it about the baby that makes it persist in learning to walk when this mode of locomotion is completely foreign to them? The answer is that there is a knowing within the baby that walking is possible. Walking is part of their DNA, and there is an innate understanding that it is something they are supposed to do.

Developing your psychic powers is much like learning to walk. Whether you are aware of it or not, the psychic potential discussed in this book is within you. It is why you were attracted to this book. It is why you are curious about this topic. Just as a baby takes small steps in its efforts to walk, your efforts in learning about psychic powers are your small steps to revealing a deeper truth of who you are.

Everything you will ever want to know or experience already exists within you as a potentiality. All it takes for that potential to be expressed is awareness and a stimulus. The baby has the potentiality to walk but it is unaware of it. It discovers that potential when it is prompted by its parents and given encouragement. Somewhere in the baby's consciousness there is a knowing that walking is possible, even if the baby is not aware of it. With each little step, the potential for walking expands, as does the awareness of that potential.

The potential for your psychic abilities has always existed within you. Though you may not consciously be aware of this potential, it will start expressing itself when the appropriate stimuli are present. At this moment, that stimulus is this book. As with any stimuli, it contains no power of its own. Instead, it elicits the power within you.

The more attention you place on the subject of psychic powers, the greater your awareness of them will become. This book's purpose is to prompt and encourage you to take the metaphysical steps that will lead you to express your psychic potential. Just as with a baby who is learning to walk, you must follow some simple but important guidelines:

Consistency and Perseverance: As it is important for babies to consistently practice, it is important for you to consistently practice developing your psychic abilities. A baby cannot learn to walk with only one day of practice. The baby needs continued practice to refine its movements, which will eventually lead to waking. Similarly, you need to consistently practice your skills to refine them until you get the results you desire.

Review Your Journal: How do parents know if their baby is making progress in walking? They compare the baby's performance with what happened in the past. In the same way, tracking your progress requires that you review your journal. This is why journaling your experiences was stressed so often in this book. You cannot know how far you have come until you understand where you were in the past.

Just as important, reviewing your journal allows you to look for patterns in your experiences. If being lost is a recurring theme in your dreams, that may be an important message from the spirit world. The more you write, the more awareness you will have of your psychic potential.

Practice with Heart: When babies learn to walk, they do not criticize or doubt themselves, though their efforts are filled with tumbles and other clumsy moments. Instead, they are driven by the encouragement of their parents. Similarly, you are bound to experience moments that do not match up to your expectations as you work on developing your psychic skills. This is a normal part of the process!

Adopt the wisdom of the baby. Be kind to yourself and know that what you are experiencing is normal and is part of your growth process. Approach your practice with a spirit of fun and curiosity rather than trying to achieve a certain outcome.

Keep on Writing: The development of your psychic abilities is an ongoing process. It is not something you do for a few months and then proclaim you have done it! Your psychic development will continue throughout this lifetime and your future lifetimes. Keep journaling. Your journaling should march side by side with your spiritual practice.

Keep on Learning: I highly recommend continuing your journey into the psychic realm by keeping up with your learning. This book was simply a basic introduction to the psychic realm; there is so much more to learn! Become a lifelong learner and continually seek out other learning resources.

Ultimately, what could be a more noble pursuit than to explore the endless potential in our minds and hearts. No other achievement can provide greater value than harnessing the unlimited power that exists within us. It is more meaningful than the acquisition of possessions, social status, or monetary wealth. All of those things are transient and will come and go.

In contrast, developing your psychic powers will expand your level of consciousness. As there is only consciousness, the expansion of your consciousness expands the collective consciousness. It is the expansion of consciousness that will create a better world for tomorrow and into the future.

Printed in Great Britain
by Amazon

86822208R00098